The Complete Guides to Horses and Ponies

HORSE & PONY TACK

Jackie Budd

Gareth Stevens Publishing
MILWAUKEE

For a free color catalog describing Gareth Stevens Publishing's list of high-quality books and multimedia programs, call 1-800-542-2595 (USA) or 1-800-461-9120 (Canada). Gareth Stevens Publishing's Fax: (414) 225-0377.

Library of Congress Cataloging-in-Publication Data

Budd, Jackie.
Horse & pony tack / by Jackie Budd.
p. cm. — (The complete guides to horses and ponies)
Includes bibliographical references (p. 64) and index.
Summary: Discusses saddles, bridles, bits, blankets, and other kinds of equipment used when riding and caring for horses and ponies, as well as their proper usage to make the animal comfortable and safe.
ISBN 0-8368-2447-4 (lib. bdg.)
1. Horsemanship—Equipment and supplies—Juvenile literature. 2. Horses—Equipment and supplies—Juvenile literature. 3. Ponies—Equipment and supplies—Juvenile literature. [1. Horsemanship—Equipment and supplies. 2. Horses—Equipment and supplies. 3. Ponies— Equipment and supplies.] I. Title. II. Series: Budd, Jackie. Complete guides to horses and ponies.
SF309.9.B84   1999
636.1'0837—dc21   99-20472

First published in North America in 1999 by
Gareth Stevens Publishing
1555 North RiverCenter Drive, Suite 201
Milwaukee, Wisconsin 53212 USA

This U.S. edition © 1999 by Gareth Stevens, Inc. Created with original © 1998 by Ringpress Books, Ltd. and Jackie Budd, P. O. Box 8, Lydney, Gloucestershire, United Kingdom, GL15 6YD, in association with Horse & Pony Magazine. All photographs courtesy of Horse & Pony Magazine. Additional end matter © 1999 by Gareth Stevens, Inc.

The publisher would like to thank Jill Groff for her assistance with the accuracy of the text. Ms. Groff has shown hunters and jumpers successfully throughout the United States and South America. Students she has trained have won competitions throughout the United States — including ribbons at prestigious horse shows, such as the National Pony Finals and the National Horse Show.

Printed in Mexico

1 2 3 4 5 6 7 8 9 03 02 01 00 99

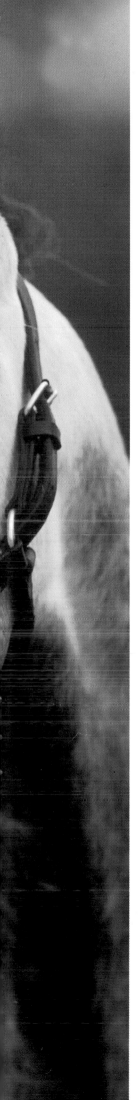

Contents

tack basics

What is tack?   4

saddles

The saddle   6
Sizing up saddles   10
Saddling up   12
Trouble spotting   14
Saddle essentials   16
Under the saddle   18

bridles & bits

Bridle basics   20
Taking up the reins   22
Simply snaffles   24
The curb family —
 Pelhams   26
The curb family —
 Double bridles   28
Gags and bitless bridles   30
Know your nosebands   32
Bridle extras   34
Putting on a bridle   36
Getting a good fit   38

A bit of a problem   40

training

Tack for training   42
Taking the lunge   44

handling

More headgear   46

horse clothing

All wrapped up   48
Which blanket?   50
Clothing to be cool
 or cozy   52

protective gear

Looking after legs   54
Bandage business   56
Traveling in style   58

tack care

Taking care of tack   60
Glossary   62
Books/Videos/
 Web Sites/Index   64

What is tack?

Snaffles, Pelhams, martingales, cruppers, coolers — horse and pony gear comes with as many names as it has straps and buckles!

All of this gear is called tack — the general name given to the items used when riding and caring for horses and ponies.

How much do you really know about tack? If you were having trouble slowing your pony down, would you know which type of bit would help? Facing a winter in the field, which blankets would you need? If you want to try endurance riding, is there a special type of saddle that would be more comfortable than others?

It is a good idea for anyone who cares for or rides horses or ponies to educate herself on all the different tack available — what it is for and how to choose and fit it properly. Finding out about tack does not mean you need to rush out and buy it all! Educated riders choose the right equipment to make life easier and safer for the horses, ponies, and themselves.

Blankets

Most ponies need one or two types of blankets, depending on their lifestyle:

♦ Ponies that go out in the field in winter need a waterproof outdoor blanket, unless they are hardy breeds that have a thick winter coat.

♦ For indoor wear, a pony needs a stable blanket.

♦ Coolers, or anti-sweat sheets, come in handy whenever a pony needs to be dried off quickly without catching a chill.

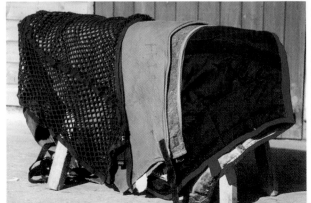

Left: **The main types of blankets are** *(left to right)* **a cooler, a turn-out blanket, and a stable blanket.**

saddle & stirrups
Position rider correctly on the pony's back

bridle
Holds the bit in the mouth

bit
Controls the pony's speed and direction through the reins

saddle pad
Goes under the saddle to absorb sweat and oil

girth
Holds the saddle in place

boots
Protect the legs, particularly when jumping

halter
For leading and tying up the pony

lead rope

basic gear

When you first get a pony, it is tempting to think you must have one of everything you see in the tack shop. In fact, most ponies manage with quite a simple wardrobe. This book points out the essentials, presenting all you need to know about using and fitting these items. Also presented is information about other equipment you may want to try in order to accomplish various activities with your pony.

The saddle

A saddle is the most expensive piece of equipment you will need to buy for your pony — and the most important. Of course, it is quite possible to ride bareback, but using a saddle is much more comfortable for the pony and for yourself. From the pony's point of view, the saddle helps put the rider in a position on his back where it is easiest and most comfortable for him to carry the weight — and keeps the rider there. The saddle holds the rider in the correct place to give signals to the pony and to stay in balance, even when the pony is moving fast or jumping.

A great invention

The saddle could be thought of as one of the greatest inventions in history. When horses were first domesticated about five thousand years ago, people rode on top of animal skins placed across the horse's back. It was not long before the idea of padding the skins, for comfort and to hold the rider steady, was born.

The first true saddles — stuffed cushions joined with leather or wooden arches — came into use about 500 B.C. Warriors with saddles were able to stay on and control their horses in battle. They could ride much longer distances than before. Riders with saddles soon defeated those without saddles.

Even the earliest saddles were designed to take weight off the horse's backbone. Wooden-framed saddles appeared in the first century, and this same design is still used today.

It is said that stirrups were first used by Attila the Hun (A.D. 400–453). Able to stand up and shoot arrows from the

what is a saddle made of?

Leather is the traditional material for making saddles. It is still by far the most commonly used, although synthetic leather-look materials *like the ones in the picture above* are becoming more and more popular. They are a good value, light to carry, and easy to keep clean.

leather saddles
♦ Have a traditional look
♦ Last a lifetime if well cared for
♦ Can be repaired and restuffed when necessary

synthetic saddles
♦ Are light to carry
♦ Can be washed
♦ Are less expensive than leather
♦ Are not as easy to repair or restuff as leather
♦ Do not stay as nice looking as leather

Above: **Visible in this interior view of a saddle are the metal stirrup bars riveted to the saddle tree. Sturdy material has been stapled over the frame to make the seat. The girth straps will be stitched onto the long strips at the front.**

saddle as they galloped, his marauding horsemen conquered a vast empire. In 1066, the use of stirrups helped the Normans defeat the Anglo-Saxons and win the Battle of Hastings.

Western and stock saddles developed from these medieval saddles. In fact, all modern saddles are based on designs once used by the military in early times.

Inside a saddle

A saddle is built around a frame called a tree. The shape of the tree is important because this is what the final shape, or "cut," of the saddle depends on. The cut influences the way the rider is positioned and the way the saddle sits on the horse. Saddles used for different purposes have different cuts. Saddle-making is a highly skilled craft requiring years of training.

The stirrup leather loops over the stirrup bar with the buckle resting on the top, as far up as it can go. Always have the safety catch down. The original idea of these catches was to keep the leather from coming away from the bar. Today, most bars are set into the saddle, keeping the leathers snugly in place. It is important that the leathers are free to come off in an emergency.

The pieces of wood joined together to make the tree are strengthened by steel plates and covered with muslin fabric. The stirrup bars, from which the stirrup leathers hang, are then riveted onto each side at the front of the tree.

The seat of a saddle is made by fastening strips of strong canvas over the tree. Three extra-long strips extend below the waist — the billets are stitched to these. The seat is stuffed, and the leather is stretched over it. Finally, the skirts are stitched over the stirrup bars, and the flaps and panels are fitted. The panels keep the rider's weight off the horse's spine and spread down each side.

The panels must be carefully stuffed to make sure there will be no pressure points and that the saddle stays in balance.

Left: A crafts-person stuffs saddle panels.

parts of the saddle

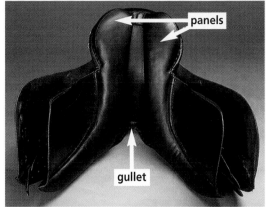

panels

gullet

billets

billet guard

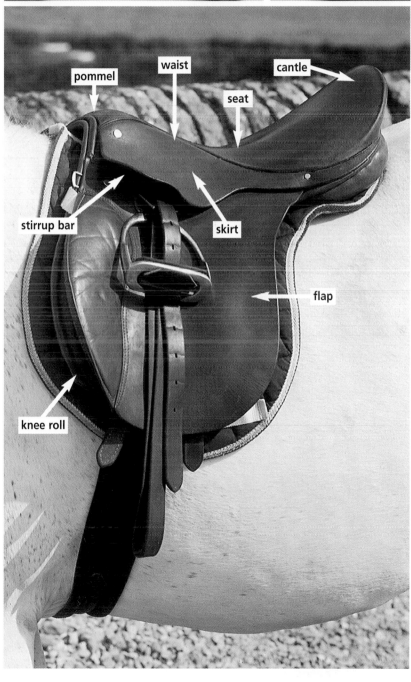

pommel

waist

seat

cantle

stirrup bar

skirt

flap

knee roll

All sorts of saddles

A hundred years ago, there was only one type of saddle available to the average rider. Unless you were a cavalry soldier or a cattle rancher, the only choice was the English hunting saddle. This saddle had a very flat seat. Because the fashion was to ride with long stirrups and lean back over a jump, the saddle had straight flaps and no knee rolls. It was very uncomfortable.

Today's saddles developed as needed for particular equestrian sports.

Below: Most riders use a General Purpose (GP) saddle.

General purpose saddle

This saddle, *shown close-up on the previous page,* is the one most modern riders use. The flaps are shaped forward a little to allow the rider to shorten the stirrups for jumping without the knee coming over the front. Knee rolls underneath give extra security over a fence. Some types have thigh rolls at the back of the panels, too.

The seat is deep to keep the rider in the center over the horse's point of balance and where his back is strongest.

Above: This jumping saddle has a forward cut to its flaps.

Jumping saddle

Showjumpers need to ride with much shorter stirrups than normal, so a saddle designed for jumping has panels and flaps that are much more forward-cut than a GP saddle. For this to work, the front, or head, of the tree has to slope backward. Jumping saddles sometimes have large knee rolls, which are sometimes put on the outside of the flap rather than underneath them.

Dressage saddle

Dressage riders sit upright and as deep as possible in the saddle with their legs almost straight. The aim is to stay in this position throughout all the paces and to be in as close contact as possible with the horse.

Dressage saddles have high, upright heads and long, straight flaps. Again, the deepest part of the seat is in the center. The panels are broader and flatter than usual, and the stirrup bars are set back under the tree so they do not poke into the rider's thighs.

Most dressage saddles have especially long billets that fasten to a special short girth below the saddle flaps. In this way, the bulky buckles are kept away from the rider's legs. Some saddles are now made with ordinary girth straps with stirrup bars and billets positioned to keep the buckles out of the way and allow for a closer "feel."

Racing saddle

Because racehorses race with as little weight as possible, and jockeys hardly ever sit in the saddle, racing saddles have hardly any seat at all. In fact, they do not even have a tree, just a flexible frame to hold the stirrup leathers.

Above: The straight flap of the dressage saddle keeps the rider's legs long and helps the rider sit deep in the saddle. Long girth straps keep the bulky buckles out of the way.

Right: Jockeys hardly ever need to sit down in their racing saddles!

Left: Endurance riding is easier with a specialized saddle.

fastened into the tree. The lower head is screwed on at a height to suit the rider. It curves over the left thigh. A special forward-cut flap on the near side keeps the rider's leg off the horse's shoulder. Like the smaller right, or off-side, flap, it is fastened down.

Western saddle

Western riding was developed by the United States cavalry and the cowboys of the American West. This uniquely American style is based on classic Spanish riding techniques. At first sight, the Western saddle seems cumbersome and elaborate, but it is really very practical. It was designed for a horse and rider spending hours, or even days, on the range.

tack tip

Sidesaddle riding is over 2,500 years old. In medieval times, the rider was seated in a kind of chair with her feet on a wooden shelf called a planchette. During the 1500s, she could hook one leg around the large, front horn of the saddle. By the end of the eighteenth century, a "leaping" head allowed women to join the hunt and take on huge hedges and fences.

Endurance saddle

Endurance riding involves many hours, even days, on the move. A saddle for this sport must be comfortable for the horse to wear as well as for the rider to sit in for long periods of time. It needs to spread the rider's weight across as large an area as possible and keep the rider in a secure, balanced position that never impedes the movement of the horse.

Endurance saddles are made with ordinary trees, making use of synthetic materials to even out pressure and increase comfort. The saddles also let the rider lean forward slightly out of the saddle if desired.

Above: Sidesaddle riding is not as dangerous as it seems. The rider's legs hook over the saddle's two heads.

Sidesaddle

Elegant sidesaddle riding is becoming popular again. The specialist saddle is a big investment because the saddles are not easy to find. New, lighter saddles are being made, but most are very old, and they are heavy and bulky.

A sidesaddle should be tailor-made to fit a particular horse and rider. It has a flat seat and is thickly padded so the rider sits up high off the horse's back. A linen lining helps absorb the horse's sweat and reduce pressure.

The rider's legs go to the near (left) side. The right leg is hooked over the top head, which is

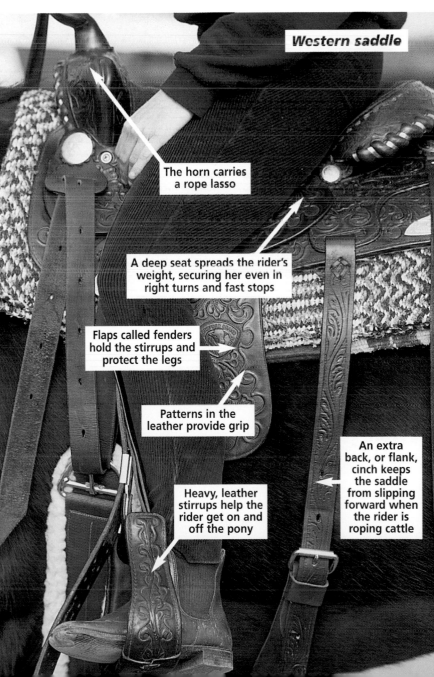

Western saddle

The horn carries a rope lasso

A deep seat spreads the rider's weight, securing her even in right turns and fast stops

Flaps called fenders hold the stirrups and protect the legs

Patterns in the leather provide grip

Heavy, leather stirrups help the rider get on and off the pony

An extra back, or flank, cinch keeps the saddle from slipping forward when the rider is roping cattle

Sizing up sad

A saddle has to fit both members of the team — you and your pony! The rider must be in the right position in the saddle and feel comfortable. The saddle must not rub or pinch the pony during the ride.

Ponies were not designed to carry weight on their backs, so a pony's saddle has to fit perfectly. For a pony that is wearing a badly fitting saddle, every stride he takes can be very painful. Making sure the saddle is always comfortable for the pony is absolutely essential.

A saddle that fits one pony perfectly is not likely to be as good a fit for his stable-mate. In addition, a pony can change shape. For example, he may go from being overweight and unfit to being lean and muscular. So even a well-fitting saddle needs to be checked regularly to be sure of a good fit.

Saddles can also change with use. The stuffing in the panels gradually squashes down, making the saddle sink too low or creating knobby areas that cause pressure. If this happens, it is time to ask a saddler to take a look. Your saddle may need to be restuffed.

get in the experts

saddle sizes

Saddles come in different lengths to suit the rider. They also come in different tree widths to suit the shape of the horse or pony.

Length is measured from the pommel across to the cantle. Saddles are usually 15 inches (38 cm) for children and 16-17 inches (40.6-43 cm) for adults. Tall or large people need even longer saddles.

Three standard-width fittings — wide, medium, and narrow — suit horses and ponies with barrels that are round, average, and narrow.

The length of a saddle is measured from the pommel to the cantle.

A good fit for the rider

Make sure that:

♦ The seat is halfway between the pommel and cantle.
♦ An adult's fist fits down the entire length of the gullet.
♦ An adult's hand width fits easily in front of and behind your body.
♦ At jumping length, your knees do not stick over the front of the flaps.
♦ At schooling length, your knees are not far away from the knee rolls.
♦ Your leathers are vertical when you are in the correct riding position (when your heels are in line with your hips).

  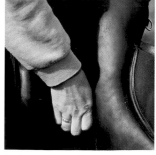

A hand's width should fit in front and behind.   **Is the gullet a fist-width?**

dles

If you are buying a new saddle, have an expert fit it to your pony. Even if a saddle came as part of the deal when you bought your pony, this does not necessarily mean it fits properly. Ask an approved saddler or a qualified instructor to check it for you.

Above: Make sure you see daylight all the way through and that you easily fit four fingers under the pommel.

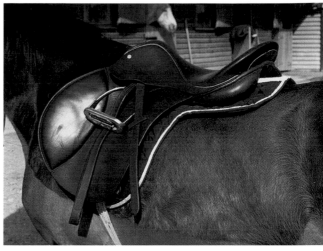

Above: This saddle is obviously too big. The flaps will get in the way of the pony's shoulders. The panels come much too far back over the loins.

A good fit for the horse

This is not quite so easy because your pony cannot speak up if the saddle is pinching. It is up to the rider to get as good fitting a saddle as possible.

Put the saddle on the pony's back, slightly forward, and slide it back, as usual *(see page 13).* Look at it without a rider first, then fastened up with a rider on board. It is not enough for the saddle to fit while the pony is standing still — he needs to be carefully looked at on the move, at all paces, and again after the workout.

Make sure that:

♦ The saddle sits level on the horse's back and is not twisted.

♦ The lowest part of the seat is midway between the pommel and cantle.

♦ You can see plenty of daylight all the way down the gullet, even when the rider is leaning forward or backward.

♦ You can easily fit four fingers between the withers and the pommel.

♦ Nothing gets in the way of the horse's movement, even when he stretches his shoulders out.

♦ The saddle does not come too far back on the sensitive loins.

♦ There is the right amount of stuffing in the panels so that the saddle stands off the horse's back.

♦ The saddle is not too low over or too spacey around the withers or able to be moved from side to side.

♦ The saddle does not sit up too high in front, pinching the withers. You should be able to slide your fingers between the saddle and the sides of the withers.

♦ The saddle does not rock forward and back when the rider is rising to the trot.

Above: Too little stuffing in the panels *(as shown),* or too much, means that pressure is focused on too small an area of the back.

Above: You should be able to slide your fingers down each side of the withers.

Above: If the saddle lifts off the pony's back each time you rise to the trot, your pony will soon be sore.

Above: Always get advice before choosing a saddle to make sure it is the best one — not just for you, but for your pony, too.

Saddling up

Carrying the saddle

Take good care of your saddle. It would cost a lot of money to replace it. A saddle can be quite heavy to carry. If you happen to drop it, it could easily be scraped on the outside or damaged on the inside.

If you need to put the saddle down, make sure it is out of your pony's reach so he doesn't step on it, chew it, or knock it off the fence or stable door. Place it up against a wall with the pommel down, resting on the cantle *(see picture at left)*. Slip the girth under the cantle so that it does not get scratched.

Left: Carrying a saddle is easy when it is done right.

when the saddle's not in use

Whenever the saddle is not being used, either on or off the pony, the stirrups should be "run up." To do this, push the iron up the back of the leather to the bar. Now, tuck the strap down through the iron. You can "run down" the irons simply by pulling them hard.

tack tip

Never leave your pony with the saddle on and the girth undone. The saddle could slip off, scaring the pony and damaging the saddle.

learn all about...
putting on saddles

1 Always tie your pony up before removing the tack. Pick up the saddle with the girth placed over the seat. Put your left hand on the pommel and your right hand under the panels. From the near side, lift the saddle and saddle pad clear of the neck. Put it gently down on the withers.

2 Slide the saddle back until the pommel is above the end of the withers. Don't push the saddle forward and ruffle up the hair. Make sure the saddle pad is pulled well up into the gullet the entire length.

3 Go around the front to the other side to let the girth down. Back at the near side, reach under the tummy for the girth. Make sure there are no twists.

4 Lift the flap and billet guard. Fasten the girth to the front two girth straps, on even holes. Check both sides to see that the front girth strap has been passed through the saddle pad loops and the girth has been passed through the bottom loop. Pull down the billet guard. This keeps the buckles from digging into the saddle flap.

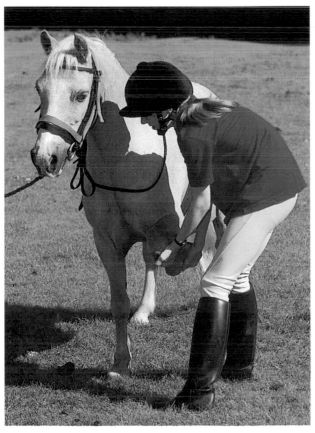

5 Don't tighten the girth too much. Tighten it one hole at a time. Keep it even on both sides. Be prepared for your pony to puff out, making the girth appear tighter than it is. Before mounting, you should be able to slide a few fingers underneath. Now stand in front of your pony and gently take hold of his foreleg under the knee. Ask him to stretch the leg forward, evening out any wrinkles of skin around the elbow. To finish, do the other side. Now you are ready to ride!

taking off a saddle

Undo the girth on the near side. Try not to drag the saddle off the back, but lift it up. Be ready to take hold of the girth as it comes over the back and place it carefully, muddy or sweaty side up, over the seat of the saddle.

tack tip *If your pony has been working hard, get off, loosen the girth, and walk him with the saddle on for a while. This helps with the circulation in his back. You could also take the saddle off and rub his back gently with your hand.*

Tension and stiffness may be saddle related.

Trouble spotting

A pony in discomfort from his saddle cannot explain this to you, but he will tell you about it in other ways. Saddle problems or back injury are not necessarily the reasons for discomfort, but they may be, especially if the problems came on suddenly. Ask your vet to check your pony thoroughly. Ask a qualified saddler to look at your tack and how it fits. Be concerned if any of the following symptoms occur:

♦ Lameness or uneven strides
♦ Stiff body or paces
♦ Short, cautious strides
♦ Neck always tense or held high
♦ Tail swishing or teeth gnashing
♦ Bucking

♦ Awkwardness about being tacked up or mounted
♦ Unwillingness to work, particularly on circles
♦ Refusing or running out at jumps or rushes
♦ Signs of bad temper, especially when the back is touched
♦ Reluctance to lie down or roll

You can sometimes tell if your pony is feeling sore if he flinches or dips when you run your fingers along his withers and back. If his hair is worn off where the panels of the saddle rest, this is another warning sign that there is too much pressure or that the saddle is moving around too much.

Left: Bucking can be horseplay — or could your pony be trying to tell you that his saddle hurts?

buying secondhand tack

If you have set your heart on a leather saddle but the price of a brand-new one is too high, look around for quality used gear. It can be found through classified ads or at a reputable saddlery shop, where there will be someone on hand to give advice.

When buying secondhand, remember to go through all the checks listed on the previous pages to make sure the saddle you have in mind is a good fit for yourself and — most importantly — for your pony. Then make some extra checks to be certain the tack is not faulty in any way:

♦ Look for scrapes and other signs of wear and tear, particularly on the billets.

♦ Check that the tree inside is not broken or weak.

♦ Tuck the cantle into your tummy and gently pull the pommel toward you *(right)*. A little give is OK, but there should not be a lot of bending, creasing, or twisting.

♦ Check the stitching. Any worn or rotting stitching *(right)* needs repairing before use.

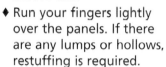

♦ Run your fingers lightly over the panels. If there are any lumps or hollows, restuffing is required.

♦ On stirrup leathers, girths, bridles, and reins, look for weak stitching, overworn holes, billet hooks, and thin or cracked areas that could snap without warning. The spots most likely to wear first are located where there is a turn in the leather, especially over metal (bit or buckle).

♦ Steer clear of inferior leather imported from the Far East.

Left: Ask your vet to check your pony's back if you have had saddle problems. A specialist in back problems may be called in to help with the treatment.

Saddle essentials

tack tips

Leathers have a habit of stretching. If you always keep them on the same side of the saddle, you will soon find the near-side one that you use for mounting is longer than the opposite one. Make a habit of switching them every time you clean your saddle, and they should stretch evenly...or you could alternate the side from which you mount.

The hole you use most often will soon get creased and worn. When this happens, ask your saddler to shorten the leathers from the buckle end.

Getting a leather through the stirrup the right way can be tricky! Hold the buckle end toward you with the smooth side of the leather upward. With the buckle, tongue down, thread the pointed end through the top of the stirrup iron. Bring it up and back and fasten it through the buckle.

To fix the leather to the saddle, push it hard over the stirrup bar. Pull down on the back piece so the buckle sits snugly up against the bar and won't dig into your leg. Tuck the spare end of leather into the loop on the flap, if the saddle has one.

Stirrup leathers

These days, stirrup leathers are often made of strong synthetic webbing instead of leather. Traditional leathers are usually made of the strongest hide because these straps take a lot of stress and strain. Buy top-quality leathers only. If an inferior strap breaks while you are riding, there could be an unfortunate accident.

Leathers come in different widths depending on whether they are going to be used with small, lightweight children's irons or with larger, heavier adult ones.

The buckles should be stainless steel.

Left: There are two things right and one thing wrong with this photo — can you spot them? Yes, instead of lying flat against the rider's leg, the stirrup leather is twisted. However, she is wearing the correct kind of footwear for riding, and the iron is the right size for her foot.

Stirrup irons

Stirrup irons should also be made of stainless steel. Heavy irons are best because they are much easier to find again if you lose your stirrup. Rubber treads that slot into the bottom of the iron help you keep your grip.

For safety, get the right size for your foot. The iron must allow about a 1/2-inch (1-cm) space on either side of your boot. Much more space than that and your foot could easily slip through, putting you in a dangerous situation.

Another thing to watch for when buying irons is to make sure the "eye" at the top is wide enough for your leathers.

Certain irons are designed to place the rider's foot at an angle to change the position of the leg, but it is best to stick with the ordinary type or a safety iron. Safety irons come in various designs that release your foot if you fall. Peacock safety irons have rubber loops.

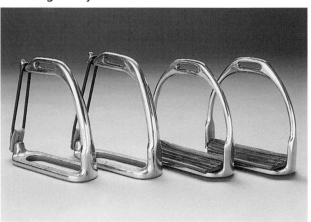

Peacock safety irons *(left)* and standard stirrup irons *(right)*.

tack tip

Always wear the right footgear for riding — something with a small heel and smooth sole. Tennis shoes, trendy shoes, or chunky-soled shoes are asking for trouble.

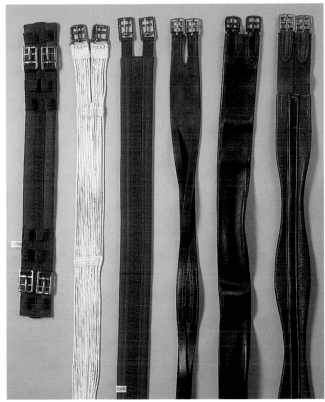

Above: Besides the ordinary straight style, girths also come in other shapes. A short belly girth is usually used with a dressage saddle. The Balding is narrow around the elbow area to keep it from digging into the elbow. The three-fold leather girth is used with the fold toward the elbow. The Atherstone is also shaped to keep the girth from digging into the elbow. *Left to right* are several girths — dressage, string, cotton-padded, Balding, three-fold, and Atherstone.

Above: Without a girth, a saddle would not stay in place for long!

Left: Some girths have elastic inserts below the buckles, or are completely elasticized. The elastic allows more give as the horse moves. This type of girth must be carefully fitted. It is popular for racehorses.

tack tip

A fleecy or sheepskin girth sleeve helps prevent rubbing and absorbs sweat.

Girths

Traditionally, girths were made of leather. Lampwick, mohair, and wool were also used. Clean leather looks beautiful. If well kept and supple, a leather girth rarely causes sores. Leather, however, can cause other problems. It lacks "give," it does not absorb sweat, and it is expensive.

Today, various synthetic materials are commonly used. Most pony owners purchase padded cotton girths, which are a good value. They are very strong, soak up moisture, and are machine washable. Old-fashioned string girths made of leather were never a very good idea. They were likely to pinch, rub, and twist or bunch up, instead of spreading pressure over a wide area like a girth should. Girth lengths vary to suit different sizes of horses and ponies. Girths range in length from about 34 inches (86 cm) to 54 inches (137 cm).

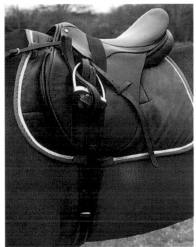

What is a surcingle?

This is a long, narrow webbing strap, sometimes stretchy, that goes around the entire saddle and under the belly. It is used in cross-country riding as an extra safety precaution just in case the girth or billets break.

Under the saddle

Saddle pads

Saddle pad is the name for an absorbent pad that is placed under a saddle. If it is rectangular in shape, it is usually called a "square" pad. The purpose of a saddle pad is to absorb some of the pony's sweat. It also keeps the underside of the saddle panels clean. The best saddle pad to use is one of the cotton quilted or cotton fleece types. They are light and easy to use. As long as they are washed regularly, they will keep soft and absorbent. Real sheepskin saddle pads look great, but they make your pony hot and sweaty. In addition, they are not very easy to clean.

The shape and size of a pad corresponds with the size of the saddle. There is a complete range of therapeutic saddle pads on the market. They are made with many kinds of natural and synthetic materials and fillings. These are designed to prevent injury and soreness by spreading the rider's weight and easing pressure. Other types of saddle pads reduce friction, draw sweat away from the back, and even massage the horse as he moves.

One of the most popular and comfortable of today's saddle pads is the type containing a gel pad.

tack tip

There's sure to be a saddle pad or cotton girth in any color these days. Fashion-conscious ponies (at the suggestion of their owners) can look pretty in pink, blue, or lime green. A more classic look, however, features the traditional colors of brown, black, or navy. White saddle pads are pretty on any pony. White girths are hard to keep clean, but they look wonderful on a gray pony.

Pull the saddle pad well up into the saddle gullet away from the backbone.

Above: This pony and rider are color coordinated during their cross-country ride.

slipping solutions

Q. What if my saddle slips backward?
A. When a horse or pony is big in the shoulder area but not as well developed behind the saddle, the saddle sometimes slips backward. A breast-plate comes in handy for this. You will often see a breastplate used by eventers or other fit horses during cross-country, where the galloping and jumping action can make the saddle shift backward.

Q. What if my saddle slips forward?
A. You may see some ponies wearing a strap that goes from a *D*-ring on the back of the saddle along the back to a padded loop around the tail *(right)*. This is called a crupper and is usually part of a driving harness. It keeps the saddle from being pushed up the pony's withers or onto the shoulders.

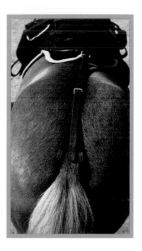

tack tip

A neckstrap is a simple leather strap around a pony's neck that gives a novice rider something safe to grab onto if she feels unsteady. An old stirrup leather makes a good neckstrap.

Above: Use all the loops to keep a saddle pad securely in place. This rider has forgotten the one for the girth.

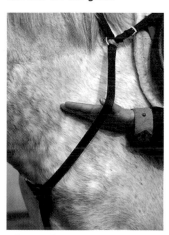

Above: This is a hunting or collar breastplate. It fastens to the *D*-rings on the front of the saddle, and goes between the legs to the girth.

Above: This breastplate fits over the withers and attaches at the sides to the billets. These are sometimes padded so they do not rub. They must fit high enough so they do not interfere with movement, but low enough to not get in the way of breathing.

The headgear worn by a horse or pony for riding is called the bridle. Most parts of the bridle are needed to hold the bit steady in the right place in the mouth. The bit and reins together help the rider stay in control of and guide the pony.

The bridle that looks most familiar is called a snaffle bridle. It is named after the type of bit that goes with it. There are other types of bridles used with other bits. Around the world, there are many different designs of bridles and bits. They are specially developed to suit particular styles of riding or types of work.

Bridles are sold in standard sizes to fit heads from Shetlands to Shires. Some of the main ones are the pony, horse, cob, and full-size. In the United States, pony, horse, and cob sizes are available.

Sometimes it is best to mix and match different-sized parts to get a good all-around fit for an individual horse or pony.

What are bridles made of?
The traditional material for bridles is leather. Tack shops now also sell bridles made of synthetic or cotton webbing. These synthetic types are easier to keep clean than leather. A washing machine does all the work. However, webbing never looks quite as attractive as traditional, elegant leather. When the pony gets sweaty, the webbing may also rub.

Parts of a snaffle bridle

head stall

browband

cheekpieces

cavesson noseband

throat-latch

reins

snaffle bit

Above: **Stainless steel is much harder wearing than the old-fashioned nickel bits. Even so, check your bit regularly for signs of wear, especially at the joints.**

Bridle basics

What are bits made of?
Top-quality bits are made of stainless steel, which is very strong and does not rust. New types of steel and other mixes of metals are also being tried. These may prove to be even stronger and more comfortable for the pony to have in his mouth.

In the past, nickel was often used. This can still be found, but never use a nickel bit. This metal is soft, bends easily, wears quickly to create sharp edges, and might snap at any time.

Racehorses have aluminum bits because aluminum is a very light metal, but it is also very weak. Bits with copper sections in the mouthpiece can often be found. The idea behind this odd-tasting, soft metal is that the horse will be encouraged to make saliva and relax his jaw.

a bit of history

The earliest riders simply used a leather rope around the horse's neck to guide him. When they wanted their horses to be more controlled, to drive in harness or to ride, bits were developed. At first, these consisted of just an extra length of rope passed through the horse's mouth. Nomadic Mongolian tribes probably made twisted rawhide mouthpieces several thousand years B.C.

Over time, humans discovered how to make and mold metals. Then, bronze, copper, and brass bits were tried. Until the twentieth century, iron was the most common metal used in the making of bits.

Some of the oldest bits were like jointed snaffles. Medieval knights, who needed instant obedience from their big, heavy horses in battle, used a bit that was shaped like a curb.

Some of the early types were incredibly heavy, bulky, and harsh. Fortunately for the horses, bits gradually became lighter and, therefore, kinder.

At the end of the 1700s, the idea came about to combine the two bits — snaffle and curb — into a double bridle, and add a curb chain.

Above: Most ponies like the warmer, softer feel of rubber or nylon bits — but they love to chew them! This Pelham has a vulcanite mouthpiece, which is sturdier than ordinary rubber.

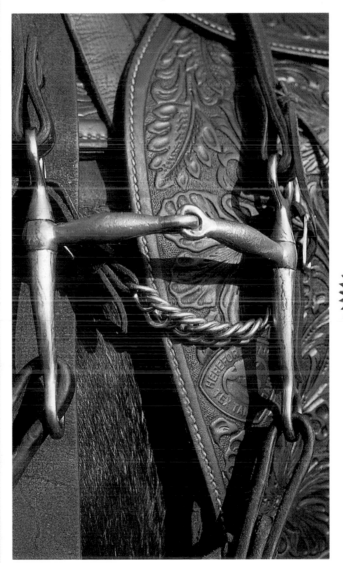

Above: Some bits have two metals in the mouthpiece. This Western bit contains copper.

tack fact

The word **bridle** comes from the Old English brigdel or bridel, derived from bregdan, which means "to pull."

tack tip

Choose a bridle that shows off your pony's best features. Make a large head appear smaller or shorter by using a noseband with a broad strap. Fasten it a few holes lower than usual. An elegant head looks best with fine straps that would seem unattractive on a big, chunky horse. In the picture above, this show cob looks beautiful in his broad-strapped bridle.

tack fact

Did you know that the craft of making bits, stirrups, and spurs is called lorinery? The Worshipful Company of Loriners received its charter from King Henry III in 1261.

Rubber mouthpieces are popular, particularly for young horses, because they are warm to the feel and bend very easily.

The problem with rubber is that ponies love to munch on it. If you use a rubber bit, watch for this and replace it if it gets too chewed. The bit should always have a metal chain or bar running through the center for safety. Vulcanite, a particularly strong, hard rubber, resists chewing much better. It is less flexible and is often used in mullen-mouth bits.

Other soft materials used in bits are lightweight nylon and plastic.

Taking up the reins

It is easy to forget that when we are riding, the reins are attached to a bit inside the horse or pony's mouth. The bit sits on his sensitive gums and presses on his tongue and lips. A good rider will always remember this and try to ride using mainly her seat and leg aids, with only a light touch on the reins.

How bits work

It is useful to learn what actually happens to the bit in the pony's mouth when you pull. The way a bit works is called its action. Each type of bit has its own action, which is why some ponies react better in some bits than in others. If you know what effect a particular bit is likely to have on your pony, you can choose the one that will suit him best.

The exact feel any bit gives a pony depends on its design. The shape of his mouth and how well he is schooled will also make a difference in how he reacts. All bits are members of one of two families — snaffles or curbs.

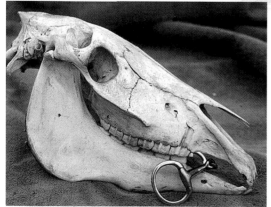

Above: In a horse or pony's mouth, there is a space between the molar, or grinding, teeth at the back and the incisor, or biting, teeth at the front. All bits lie across this gap, called the bars, in the mouth.

How snaffle bits work

When a rider puts pressure on a snaffle through the reins, the bit pushes down on the corners of the pony's lips, the tongue, and the gums.

Straight-bar snaffles press directly on the tongue, so thick-tongued horses or ponies would be better off with a jointed or at least a mullen-mouth snaffle.

When a rider pulls on the rings of a single-jointed snaffle, the joint pushes up toward the roof of the pony's mouth. Pressure lifts off the tongue but comes down on the gums and lips.

Even though the snaffle is thought to be gentle, a rider with rough hands can still easily hurt a pony's mouth by making the bit crunch onto the sensitive gums or jab upward.

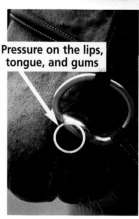

Pressure on the lips, tongue, and gums

Above: A snaffle bit acts on the corners of the pony's lips, the tongue, and the gums.

Below: Use as soft a touch on the bit as possible. Regular lessons will help you. Instead of relying on the reins, you can be in perfect balance and in control of your pony mainly by using your body weight and leg aids.

Double-jointed snaffles also press on the gums and lips but don't have such a strong squeezing action. There is not as much room for the tongue, either. If the center link has a straight edge or is set at an angle (like in a Dr. Bristol snaffle), this can dig into the tongue and be quite severe.

Whenever a pony feels pressure from a bit on the corners of his mouth, he will lift his head to avoid that feeling. That is why snaffle bits are said to have a raising action; they tend to make the horse or pony gather his entire body up.

How curb bits work

Curb bits have a much more powerful effect than snaffles. Besides working on the tongue, gums, and lips, they also put pressure on the horse's poll (behind his ears) and his jaw. So you must be gentle and more careful than ever with your hands.

Why are curb bits so strong?

This is because of the long side pieces, called cheeks, and the curb chain. If the rein attached to the bottom of the cheek is pulled, the cheek acts like a lever. This

creates a huge amount of pressure inside the mouth. It also pulls down on the cheekpieces of the bridle, which tightens into the headpiece going over the pony's sensitive poll area. This means that pressure is put onto the head at the same time.

Add to this the effect of the curb chain, and you can see that a pony wearing a curb is getting pushed in all directions. As the cheek of the bit comes back, the curb chain is lifted up into the soft chin area, squeezing the bottom jaw. This makes the horse bend more at the poll and bring his nose in closer to his chest. If it is being used in the right way, the curb bit encourages him to relax his jaw, neck, and back, and take more weight onto his hindquarters.

A rider using a double bridle should have only the very lightest of contacts on the rein attached to the curb bit. She will ride mainly using the snaffle.

Above: The bit cheek acts like a lever when pressure is put on the bottom rein. That is how a curb bit works. It pulls down on the bridle cheekpiece, pressing on the poll. The curb chain rises up in the chin's curb groove. Add this to the pressure of the bit on the tongue, the gums, and the lips, and you can see why it has a more powerful action than the simple snaffle.

Right: Some ponies do well in a curb bit like a Pelham, but others object to the action of the curb chain and might be reluctant to go forward. Make sure you always ride with as light a contact as possible.

Simply snaf

Why do most horses and ponies wear snaffles?
This bit is popular because horses and ponies, if they have been well taught, do well in it. It fits most mouths and, as long as the rider is not pulling or jerking on the reins, it is not harsh on the pony.

The snaffle is used for training a pony and rider because it is comfortable for the pony but allows the aids to be given clearly. As long as the rider is using all the aids correctly — not only the reins but her legs and seat, too — it also encourages the pony to hold his head in the right position.

If you are not sure what bit to use with your pony, the best choice is probably a snaffle.

common single-jointed snaffles

There are three basic designs of snaffles, but there are many variations within each design. Four common single-jointed snaffles are pictured *below*.

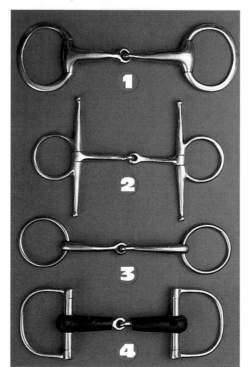

1 Eggbutt: the rings join the mouthpiece at a fixed *T*-junction. The bit is held still in the mouth.

2 Full cheek: the cheeks may be above and below the ring, or just above it. They help with steering. To keep this bit at the right angle in the mouth, the cheeks fasten to the bridle cheekpieces with leather keepers. This angle makes a cheeked bit sit higher. It has a stronger action than a bit without cheeks because it acts like a lever.

3 Loose-ring: the bit rings move through a hole in the mouthpiece. This helps the pony relax his jaw, but be careful that it fits well, has not worn sharp, and does not rub or nick his lips.

4 *D*-ring: this bit helps with steering. The straight edge pushes against the side of the face and stops the ring from going into the mouth on a tight turn. Racing bits have *D*-rings.

fles

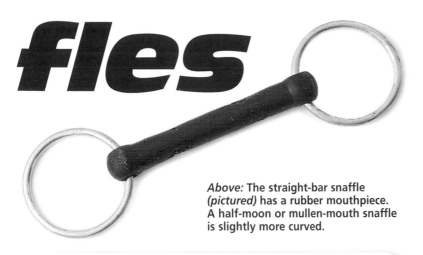

Above: The straight-bar snaffle *(pictured)* has a rubber mouthpiece. A half-moon or mullen-mouth snaffle is slightly more curved.

two double-jointed snaffles

5 French-link (cheeked): the plate in the center is shaped like a figure eight and sits comfortably on the tongue. Ponies usually like this bit.

6 Dr. Bristol: it has a flat plate, which is set at an angle. Make sure you correctly place it in the pony's mouth. If the lower edge is pointing backward, it digs down and back into the pony's tongue when the rein is pulled. This is a more severe action than when the edge is angled forward.

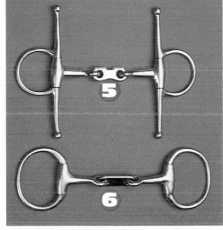

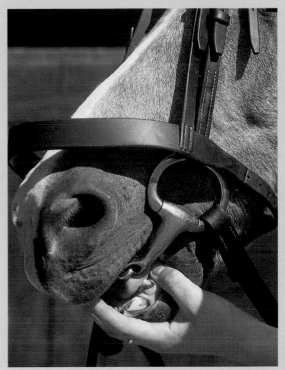

A thick eggbutt is gentle. Thick mouthpieces work best for young horses and ponies.

Thick or thin?

The number of joints in the bit and how the rings attach to the mouthpiece are two ways that the design of the bit changes the effect. Another is the thickness of the mouthpiece.

All bit styles can be purchased with thicker or thinner mouthpieces. The thinner the mouthpiece, the more control the rider has. Thicker mouthpieces are usually used for young horses and ponies and inexperienced riders because the pressure on the tongue and lips is spread out more.

The size of a pony's mouth must be considered when choosing a bit. A pony with a small mouth or jaw cannot be expected to wear a huge, thick bit.

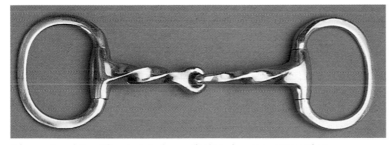

Above: Any bit with a twisted mouthpiece has a severe action.

Other sorts of snaffles

There are dozens of unusual snaffles. Some may have many joints in them, not just one or two. They might have movable rollers set into the mouthpiece to keep the horse or pony from being able to take hold of the bit and pull on it. Others have twisted or grooved mouthpieces that focus the pressure into a very narrow area that is sharp on the tongue.

Most of these bits are for historic study only and so severe they would probably stop a charging rhinoceros — so you can imagine how miserable they felt in a pony's mouth. In modern times, they are never suitable for use.

Left: This is not a cheeked snaffle — it is a Fulmer. It is useful for young horses because the cheeks help guide the horse. The loose rings allow the bit to move freely in the mouth.

The curb family — Pelhams

Besides snaffles, the other common type of bit you may see is a type of curb bit called a Pelham. Curb bits have a much stronger action than snaffles. If you see a pony with a Pelham on, you know that he is probably quite an exciting ride or does not respond well to a gentle bit.

The Pelham works like a double bridle but is much simpler to wear and use because it has only one mouthpiece. It is useful for strong, chunky ponies that may have a young or novice rider.

Because the Pelham is a curb bit, it is more powerful than a snaffle. Harsh hands can do a lot of damage with any bit that uses a curb chain, even if you are using only a single rein. *See page 29* for how to properly fit any bit with a curb chain.

See page 29

tack tip

There is no point using a Pelham without its curb chain — you may as well just use a straight-bar snaffle!

Left: Strictly speaking, a Pelham should use two separate reins — one attached to the top ring like a snaffle and the other on the bottom to make the curb chain work when more control is needed. This Pelham has a mullen-mouth vulcanite mouthpiece like the one pictured on *page 21*.

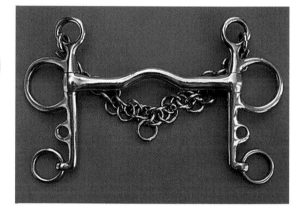

Above: There are many varieties of Pelhams. Most have a straight mouthpiece, although some have a small bump. The bigger the bump, the stronger the bit, because it presses into the roof of the mouth.

Above: Pelhams can also be jointed. Notice where the lip strap attaches.

Right: This is a Kimblewick, a kind of Pelham bit. It works like a snaffle when the hands are carried normally, just above the withers. If the rider lowers her hands, the reins slip to the bottom of the *D*-rings and the curb action comes into play. Fitting the curb chain properly is crucial.

Left: This picture shows the correct use of a Pelham with two reins.

Above: In Western riding, a snaffle bit may have long shanks like a curb and be used with a curb strap or chain. It is often described as a reining horse bit and allows for a very light touch to be used.

The curb family —
Double brid

The elegant double bridle

The double bridle is the most elegant and sophisticated of all bitting arrangements. It is to be used only by the most skillful riders on the most well-trained and educated horses to fine-tune their performance.

Sometimes you see people using double bridles when all they want is to stop their horse quicker or to look elegant. Often these riders have no idea how the two bits work in their horse's mouth. Using a double bridle wrongly or roughly can cause a great deal of pain and discomfort for the horse or pony. It is crucial to use a double bridle properly — or not at all.

The two bits of a double bridle must be positioned properly in the mouth to work and be comfortable for the horse or pony. The rider can use them to give very sophisticated and subtle signals to a horse or pony that understands these aids.

The rider must have super-sensitive hands and be able to use each rein separately from the other. Most of the time, the only contact is on the bridoon (snaffle) rein to guide the horse and ask for the correct head position.

Occasional light touches on the curb rein ask the horse to become more collected. The rider must never pull on either rein or use them both at once.

fitting a curb chain

A curb chain has to fit so that it lies smoothly in the pony's chin groove.

1 Make sure the hooks are hanging down straight. Now straighten out the chain so that it is completely flat and the ring (fly link) for the lipstrap is underneath.

2 Hold the chain in your right hand with your thumb upward. Slip it onto the offside hook so that when it is twisted clockwise, the upper part of the link that is on the hook will be on the inside of the hook.

3 On the pony's near side, twist the chain until it is completely flat. Take the end in your right hand with your thumb on the outside of the last link. Keeping your fingers on the inside between the chain and the pony, put the last link on the near side hook with your thumbnail up, without letting go.

4 If the chain is too loose, you will need to put another link on, too. Slip your fingers down to the next link you want to attach. With your thumbnail down, attach that to the hook.

5 The lipstrap buckles to the little ring on the offside cheek of the bit and goes through the fly link.

Curb chains

Curb chains range from single-link ones, which tend to pinch or rub the horse or pony's chin, to the more comfortable and better-looking double-link chains.

You can buy rubber guards to cover metal chains. Also available are chains actually made of rubber or elastic on leather. These are softer to wear but can get sweaty underneath and rub.

Above: As its name says, the double bridle is two bridles in one — it has two bits and two sets of reins. There is a small, thin snaffle called a bridoon that carries a slightly thicker rein. The most common type of curb used is the Weymouth *shown here*. The longer the cheeks or shanks of the curb, the stronger the bit because it acts like a lever. An extra strap called a slip-head is needed on a double bridle to carry the bridoon bit.

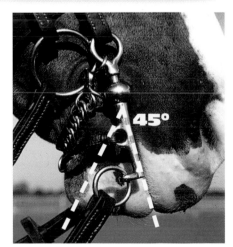

Above: If the curb chain is too tight, it will put pressure on the pony's chin groove almost all the time. Too loose, and it might as well not be there. The curb chain comes upward into the chin groove when the cheeks of the bit are brought to about a 45° angle to the lips.

Gags and bitless bridles

There are a couple of other kinds of bridles you may come across — gags and bitless bridles. One sounds cruel, the other sounds kind. As you read on, however, you will see that things are not always as they seem!

What is a gag?

Gag snaffles have a reputation for being used on very hard-pulling horses that take off with their riders. A gag is a powerful bit, but it is actually no harsher than a curb. It can be useful for a horse or pony that gets too frisky, especially cross-country.

The idea of the gag is to slow the horse down and, at the same time, ask him to raise his head up. It usually has a single-joint and works as a normal snaffle but also puts some pressure on the poll.

The gag is good for the kind of pony that insists on galloping along with his nose tucked into his chest or on the floor.

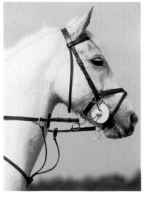

Left: The traditional gag snaffle, known as a Cheltenham gag, has holes in the top and bottom of the bit rings. A special cheekpiece passes through the bit to the reins. When the rein is pulled, the ring moves up in the horse's mouth. To be correct, an extra rein should attach directly to the bit ring so the gag rein is used only in an emergency.

Two other gags that have become popular for jumping are the Dutch gag *(left)* and the American gag *(above)*. These use ordinary bridle cheekpieces that attach to the top ring. The reins are fitted to the lower rings. Both these bits should be used with two reins, although many riders use only one.

Bitless bridles

A bitless bridle is always handy to have around if a pony has a sore mouth for any reason. Some horses wear one all the time if a regular bit is uncomfortable. Bitless bridles are also popular in the sport of endurance riding, where horses wear their tack for many hours and a bit would get in the way of drinking.

You might think that a rider could not possibly have control over a horse or pony without a bit in his mouth — but that is not necessarily true. A horse or pony that is well schooled will react to the rider's seat and leg aids and not rely on signals to the bit.

A trained Western horse will perform the most intricate of movements at all speeds in a bridle without a bit or with barely any contact at all on his mouth.

Above: Pictured is a Scawbrig bridle. This bitless bridle is suitable for a novice rider, but not all types are mild. Some types put a great deal of pressure on the horse's nose, jaw, and poll.

Above and right: This bridle is often called a hackamore, but it is actually a Blair pattern bitless bridle. It comes in two types. The English type *(above)* has broad metal cheeks and often has a sheepskin padded noseband. The German type *(right)* has longer, thinner cheeks, and the noseband can be quite narrow. The lever action of the long cheeks crunches down on the nose, while the cheekpieces pull on the poll, and the curb strap comes up onto the jaw. It works in a similar way to a curb bit but with much more force on the nose. Fit the noseband high enough so that it does not interfere with breathing.

tack fact

The word **hackamore** comes from the Spanish word *acquima*. This was a device that controlled a horse by putting pressure on the nose and jaw bones. It was invented in medieval times by the Moors.

Above: The true hackamore is a rope bridle used in Western equitation. It is based on a thick, plaited noseband called a bosal, which is balanced under the jaw by a heel knot where the reins attach.

Why bother with a noseband?

There is no rule that says a bridle has to include a noseband. In some forms of riding, such as Western, horses do not wear them. However, if you ride English, a noseband with the bridle completes the picture.

The simplest form of noseband is the cavesson, *pictured at left*. It is a plain band of leather held in place by a long strap that passes between the ears and then buckles under the jaw. The cavesson fits loosely above the bit, about midway between the edges of the cheekbones and the corners of the mouth.

The cavesson does not affect the performance of the horse or pony, but it is useful for attaching a standing martingale.

What other nosebands are there?

Plain cavesson nosebands suit most well-behaved ponies. Some horses and ponies, however, escape the action of the bit by opening their mouths wide. There are several types of nosebands designed to persuade them to keep their mouths closed so that the bit can work properly. These nosebands fit below the bit, rather than above it.

The important thing about using these drop-type nosebands is to get the fit right. Horses and ponies have to breathe through their nostrils — they do not breathe through their mouths. A noseband that is fitted too low will press down on the nostrils. This not only prevents the pony from being able to take full breaths, it can also panic him and, not surprisingly, make him behave poorly.

tack fact

The **drop-type noseband** *is a newcomer. When horses were mainly used for work and in the army, no one worried about open mouths. When equestrian sports became popular, however, these nosebands helped improve performances.*

Right: This is a drop noseband. It is not often seen in modern times, but it was once very popular. It should be fitted well up on the bony part of the nose, almost as high as the cavesson. Leave at least three fingers' width between the strap and the nostrils.

Know nose

Right: The flash noseband is a cavesson with an extra strap that is either stitched or slips through a loop at the front, on top of the nose. The flash strap fits below the bit, buckling just under the chin. Do not fit it too low. Have the cavesson strap a little lower than normal or the lower strap will drag it forward. A standing martingale can be used with the flash, attached to the cavesson strap. A martingale should never be fastened to a drop noseband strap.

Above: This is a Grakle, or figure-eight, noseband. It consists of two thin straps that cross in a figure eight at the front of the nose. It fastens under the jaw, with the lower strap fitting below the bit. The straps have to be snug if they are going to keep the horse from opening his mouth. Make sure the Grakle is not too tight or placed so high that it rubs the bones of the face. The flash and Grakle should only be used with a snaffle. Using these nosebands with a curb bit is unfair to the pony.

your bands

tack fact

Grakle nosebands are not allowed in dressage competition, except for the dressage phase in horse trials. They are often seen on racehorses and event horses because the noseband sits up high and lets the nostrils open wide during fast work.

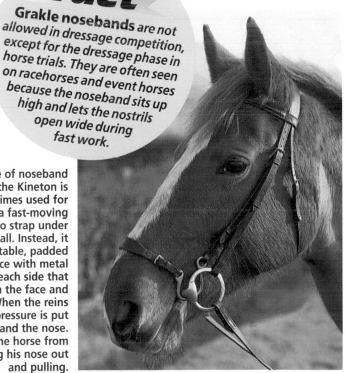

tack tip

Can you fit a finger or two easily underneath your drop, flash, or Grakle noseband? All the way around? If not, it is fastened too tightly!

Right: A type of noseband called the Kineton is sometimes used for "brakes" on a fast-moving pony. It has no strap under the chin at all. Instead, it has an adjustable, padded nosepiece with metal loops on each side that fit between the face and the bit. When the reins are pulled, pressure is put on the bit and the nose. This keeps the horse from sticking his nose out and pulling.

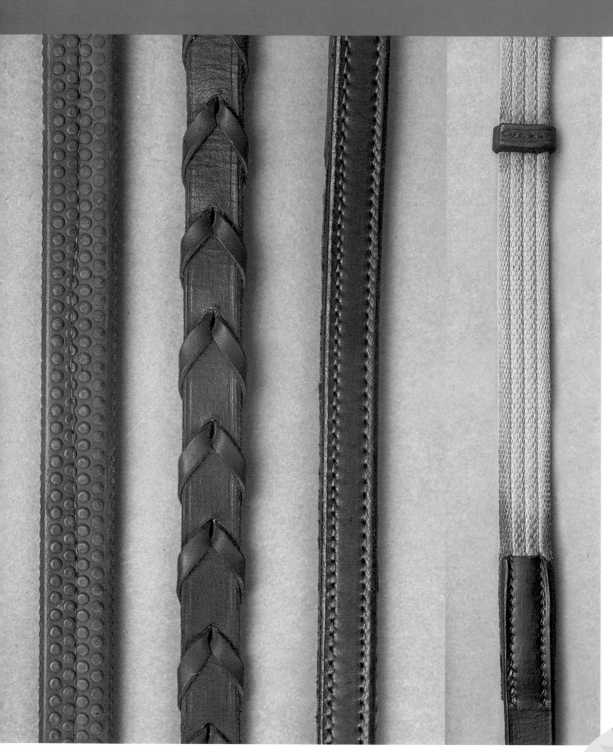

Choose your reins

rubber-covered
Best for hunting and cross-country because rubber has a good grip. Not as good for dressage because the hands cannot feel or adjust reins easily.

laced or plaited leather
Good for jumping and cross-country because they have grip even when wet.

plaited cotton/nylon
Harsh on the rider's hands, and they stiffen.

plain leather
Always used for showing and best for dressage.

continental
Leather loops at intervals for grip. Difficult to move the hands along.

tack fact

Ever wondered why reins are split and buckled in the middle? It dates from the time when cavalry horses had to be left standing in rows, with each rein unbuckled and attached to the horse next in line.

Bridle extras

Reins

Reins come in pairs that buckle together at the ends where the rider holds them. The other ends fasten to the bit with a strong fastener that is easy to use and very safe.

It is not true that one pair of reins is much like another. How the reins feel in your hands will make a difference in how you handle them, your feel on the bit, and the way you give hand aids.

The width, length, style, and material of the reins all make a difference. Choose a width for your bridle that suits the size of your hands. Small hands need narrow reins of about 1/2 inch (1-1.25 cm) wide. Bigger hands need a width of about 3/4-1 inch (2-2.5 cm).

Don't buy reins that are too long for your pony. Overly long reins are dangerous! Most pony reins are around 4 feet (1.2 meters) long. Some reins reach 5 feet (1.5 m).

Above: Plowmen, carters, and brewers decorated their horses' harnesses with beautiful ornamental brasses, originally used as lucky charms to ward off evil. Each brass figure had a special meaning — the shape of the Sun, for example, meant good fortune.

Below: There are plenty of browbands to choose from. Select your favorite colors, coordinate with your cross-country gear, or choose a traditional clincher browband with brass or gold insets.

Above: Pictured is an Australian cheeker noseband. Bit guards stretch up to the nose and continue in one strip up to the bridle headpiece like an upside-down *Y*. With a strong horse, it keeps the bit up in the mouth and keeps him from getting his tongue over it.

Above: Western tack looks beautiful.

Above: Rubber bit guards, or biscuits, can be fitted between the bit ring and the mouth so there is no chance of rubbing or pinching. They also keep the bit from being pulled through the mouth during a tight turn.

Above: Ouch! This is a brush pricker or bit burr. It is used like a bit guard but on one side only. The goal is to get the horse moving away from that side. It helps steer a horse that leans continually on one side of the bit.

Putting on a bridle

Putting on a bridle looks easy — until you try it! Getting this job done correctly takes practice, particularly if your pony likes to put his nose up in the air out of reach. As long as the bit is comfortable and the bridle itself also fits your horse or pony well, most horses and ponies will allow the bridle to be put on without much of a fuss. Take great care when putting on and taking off the bridle, though, because a pony's mouth and ears are sensitive. Rough or careless handling can soon make a pony head-shy.

Watch out for your own fingers, too — it is easy for a pony to accidentally bite them because you put them right inside his mouth.

1 It is best to tack up in a stable or other enclosed space. (These photos were taken outside to make it easier for you to see). Before starting, make sure the bridle throat-latch and noseband are undone. Stand alongside the pony's near side, facing forward. Put the reins over the pony's head.

2 Put your right hand under the jaw and up onto the nose to help control the head. Use this hand to hold the bridle, so the bit is in front of the mouth, against the teeth. Use your left hand to guide the bit in. You may need to slip your thumb carefully into the side of the gums to encourage him to open up.

3 Carefully bring the head-piece up and over the ears by gently bending the ears. Now pull the forelock through and smooth the mane flat.

4 Buckle the throat-latch. Check that the cheekpieces are lying over the noseband on both sides. Fasten the noseband and make sure it is sitting straight. Also make sure the bit and bridle are properly adjusted.

tack tip

Finished tacking up? Don't leave your pony loose in the stable with the reins dangling — it would only take a second for him to get a foot through, start munching on the leather, or even roll! Put the halter on over the bridle like this and tie him up. The reins can be passed under the run-up stirrups for extra security until you are ready to ride.

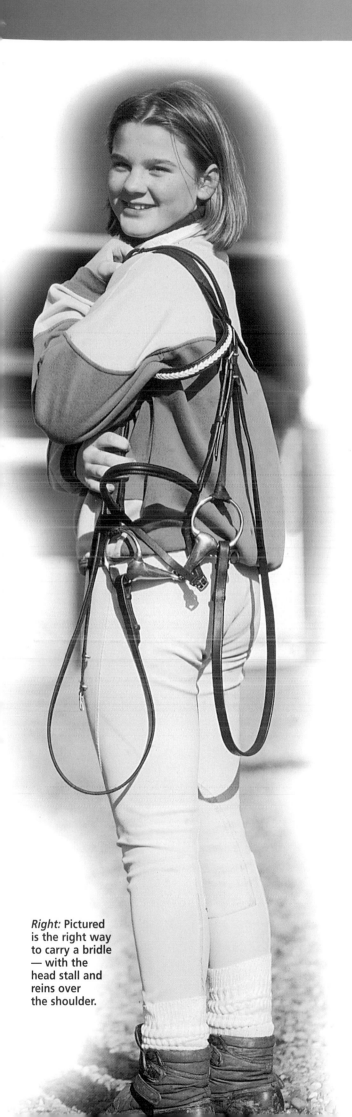

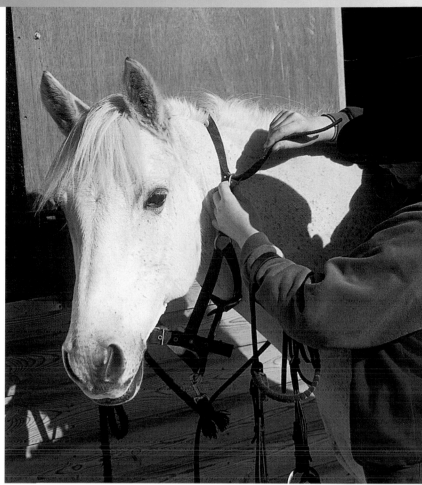

Above: If you are tacking up outside, always keep hold of your pony. You can undo the halter and fasten it around his neck, like this, while you put the bridle on. Make sure that the pony does not put his head down and choke or get tangled in the gear. Never leave your pony alone with the halter only fastened around the neck.

Right: There are two ways to neatly put away a bridle in the tack room. Thread the reins through the throat-latch, buckle it, and fasten the noseband around the entire bridle — or fasten the throat-latch in a figure eight, like this.

tack tip

Would you like a lump of freezing cold metal in your mouth? Neither does your pony! If your tack is kept in an outbuilding and is freezing cold, dip the bit in some warm water to take the chill off before putting on the bridle.

Right: Pictured is the right way to carry a bridle — with the head stall and reins over the shoulder.

taking the bridle off

Stand alongside your pony. Always undo the throat-latch and the noseband. Bring the reins up to the ears. Take the reins and headpiece in your right hand, and lift the bridle carefully over the ears and off. Use your left hand to support the bit as it comes out of the mouth, so you don't knock it against the pony's front teeth.

Getting a good fit

Throat-latch
Don't fasten the throat-latch too tightly. Leave enough space for four fingers between the strap and the pony's cheek.

Browband
This should be big enough, but not droopy. If it is too tight, it will pull the headpiece forward onto the base of the ears behind. It could also pinch the front of the ears.

Above: A cavesson should sit midway between the pony's facial bones and the corners of his mouth.

Noseband
You should easily fit two fingers all the way around the noseband (one finger for a drop-type). A cavesson should sit midway between the pony's facial bones and the corners of his mouth.

Bit
Any badly fitting bit can be very uncomfortable for a pony. This will also keep your signals from getting through to him. A bit should just wrinkle the sides of the mouth. There should be no more than 1/4 inch (0.5 cm) of mouthpiece showing between the rings and the lips on each side. Then it will lie on the bars of the gums without touching the teeth, and it will work on the appropriate areas of the mouth. Adjust the height of the bit by altering the cheekpiece buckles.

Above: Throat-latch and browband.

Above: Noseband.

Above: Fitting the bit too low is another mistake. This pony is hurting. His noseband is too low, and the huge bit must be clanking on his teeth with the point of the joint jabbing into the roof of his mouth.

Above: This bit is too small.
Below: Ouch! A bit needs to sit well up in the mouth, but not this high!

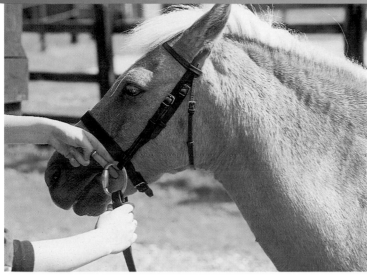

Above: If you can just fit a finger between the rings and the pony's face, the bit size is about right.

tack tip

If you are not sure what size bit your pony needs, borrow a few to try on him. Measure the one that fits him best, and ask your saddler for one in that size.

bit sizes

A horse or pony should never wear a bit that is too big or too small. Every type of bit can be bought in any size, ranging from 4-4 1/2 inches (10-11 cm) for tiny ponies to 5 inches (13 cm) or more for large horses. The measurement is the length of the mouthpiece, not including rings.

putting a bridle together

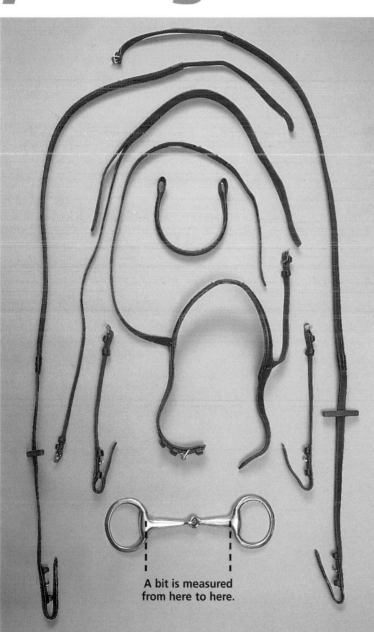

A bit is measured from here to here.

Practice taking apart and putting a bridle together.

1 Lay all the pieces out so you can clearly see what is there.

2 Hold the browband as if it's on a pony facing you. Thread the head stall up through the left loop and down through the right.

3 Thread the noseband through the browband loops so it lies underneath the head stall, and then fasten it.

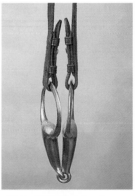

4 Buckle the cheek-pieces to their ends (on the head stall). Fasten the bit to the cheekpieces, making sure it is the right way up.

5 Attach the reins to the bit so the hooks are on the inside. Buckles face outward. Billet hooks on the cheekpieces and reins face inward.

"Hey, come down here!"

A bit of probl

When we canter or jump, my pony gets very excited. He leans on the bit and pulls. I have been told to change to a stronger bit. Which would be best?

Being in control is important to enjoying your riding and staying safe. Sometimes it is better to use a bit with a strong action and keep only a light touch on the reins.

Getting tough with an over-enthusiastic pony and resorting to a stronger bit is not always the answer, however. Take lessons to learn to steady your pony using your seat and body rather than pulling on the reins. It is a sure thing that if you pull, your pony will pull back, whatever bit you use. Changing to a milder bit often works better than using a stronger one. Sometimes a change of noseband or adding a martingale is enough to give you the control you need.

If you decide to change bits, ask your instructor's advice first. She will be able to suggest which to try and show you how to use them properly.

I have trouble steering around a showjumping course. What sort of bit would help?

Bits with cheeks help with steering because, as the rein on one side is pulled, the opposite cheek presses against the pony's face to guide him that way. Using bit guards or a bit with *D*-shaped rings can also make a difference.

Remember not to rely just on your reins and the bit at the end of them to make a turn. Slow down — if you are going too fast, your horse or pony will be the one in control, not you, so anything can happen.

Prepare for each turn in plenty of time, looking in the direction you want to go. Use your seat and body weight to steady your horse or pony, and your legs to help guide him around the turn, in balance.

My pony sticks his head in the air when I try to put his bridle on. What can I do?

During placement of the bridle, some horses and ponies wave their heads around so high you need a ladder.

One answer is to find something safe and secure to stand on. Another trick is to undo the reins, slip one under the neck and buckle them up again so you have the reins around the neck. Now take them up to behind the ears, take hold of them under the jowl, and use them to keep the head down. You can then put the headpiece of the bridle over the pony's nose.

Don't forget that your pony could be trying to tell you his bridle or bit is uncomfortable or his teeth hurt. Or maybe you are not using your hands very sensitively when you are riding. Ask an instructor to help you make sure your position and aids are right.

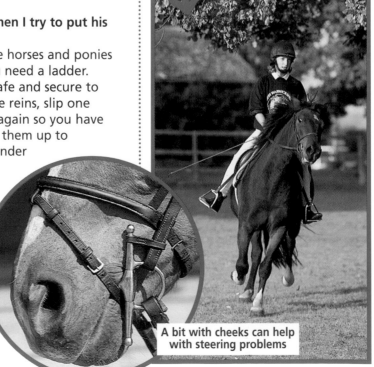
A bit with cheeks can help with steering problems

a em

Check the rules to be sure which bits are allowed for dressage

I would like to do some novice dressage tests. What bit can I use?
Even if the dressage competition you are going to is not affiliated (that is, registered with a national association), it will probably use the same rules as if it were. The rules state that novice competitors must ride in a snaffle bit. The bit can be straight, single or double-jointed (though not a Dr. Bristol), and it can have a rubber, nylon, or metal mouthpiece. Because snaffles are the only bit allowed, it is best to do all your schooling in a snaffle. Double bridles are used only by advanced horses and riders. Pelhams are not allowed in dressage.

teeth trouble

Teeth are important for all horse and pony owners and riders to know about. Head-tossing, getting the tongue over the bit or fighting against it, bucking, refusing to be bridled — many riding problems are caused by teeth that have not been properly cared for. That's not even mentioning how sharp teeth can cause feeding problems and make a pony lose weight, too.

Why do the teeth get sharp? A pony is a grazing animal, designed to grind up grasses all day long, with a forward-back scrunching action of the jaws. Therefore, his teeth are growing all the time — otherwise they would soon wear out on each other. Although the centers wear down evenly, the outside edges of the upper molars and the inside edges of the bottom molars do not. Sharp edges soon develop and cut into the inside of the pony's cheek, especially when a bit is put into the mouth.

Ask your vet to file these edges smooth. This should be part of your routine, with a check every six months.

Some ponies also grow tiny little teeth on the top jaw where the bit lies. These "wolf" teeth should be removed by the vet.

Tack for training

Martingales

Many horses and ponies have discovered how easy it is to ignore what the rider is asking them to do by sticking their noses up in the air. Anyone who has ever ridden a pony that flings his head up knows how this can lead to him getting out of control.

Many ponies wear martingales to give the rider a little extra help. Don't put a martingale on your pony just because you think it looks good. Use one only if your instructor advises you that your pony needs it. There are two main types:

Running

This is made up of a neckstrap that holds a strap that goes between the legs to the girth. It splits to make two straps with rings that the reins pass through. Notice the rubber ring that holds the neckstrap in place to keep it from drooping, and the "stops" on the reins to prevent the rings from sliding up and catching on a tooth or the bit. The running martingale keeps the bit in the right place if the pony's head goes up. If it is fitted correctly, it will only come into action when the head is raised too far.

Standing

These were once very popular, then were thought of as old-fashioned and unfair. Now they are making a comeback. Properly fitted, they do keep a pony from throwing his head up dangerously without pulling on the mouth. The neckstrap supports a plain strap that goes from the girth directly to a cavesson noseband.

tack fact

The idea for the standing martingale came from the polo players of the Indian Raj, who found a turban cloth very handy for tying between the noseband and girth to keep the polo ponies' heads down. It could easily be shortened by knotting it.

learn *all* about... martingales

Left: Don't fit a running martingale too tight, or there will be constant pressure on the mouth. The rings should reach to within a hand's width of the pony's withers above when laid against the shoulder, *as shown.*

Left: Fastened too tightly, the standing martingale will only encourage the pony to lean on it. The strap should be able to be pushed almost right up under the pony's throat, *as shown.*

Left: Whichever martingale you use, a hand's width should fit under the neckstrap.

Above: Another martingale is the Market Harborough. It is a rein and martingale in one. It brings the horse's head down if he tries to fling it up. If the horse flings his head in the air, this martingale exerts strong pressure on the rein and bit.

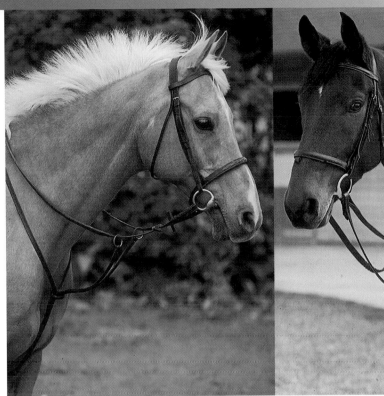

Above: Martingales help the rider keep better control of a horse or pony that tries to avoid the action of the bit by raising his head. *At left* is a running martingale; *at right* is a standing.

Training reins

You may see professional riders and trainers using many kinds of straps, gadgets, and devices. For instance, draw reins (which loop from the girth through the bit rings to the rider) and the type of reins that loop around the poll and feed through the bit rings to the hands are two such training aids. The de Gogue, Chambon, and Abbot Davies balancing reins are examples of others.

Bad reputation

Some gadgets have a bad reputation, although the devices themselves are not usually at fault. The problem comes from the rider who uses the gadgets wrongly or unnecessarily. For an expert rider who is dealing with a young, difficult horse or a highly trained horse, aids like draw reins can speed up training, develop suppleness, and avoid arguments by communicating to the horse or pony exactly what the rider wants.

Problems start when an inexperienced rider tries draw reins or another gadget to try to get instant results or even just to look "cool." Simply pulling on the reins will create one very stiff, uncomfortable horse that is only learning to lean on the bit. He may even object to all this restriction — and then the rider has real trouble on her hands!

It is best to leave training gadgets to the experts. Maybe someday that will be you — a sensitive and effective rider who knows all about special equipment and how and when to use it.

Above are draw reins, and *below* is a device called a Harbridge. These devices are best left to the experts.

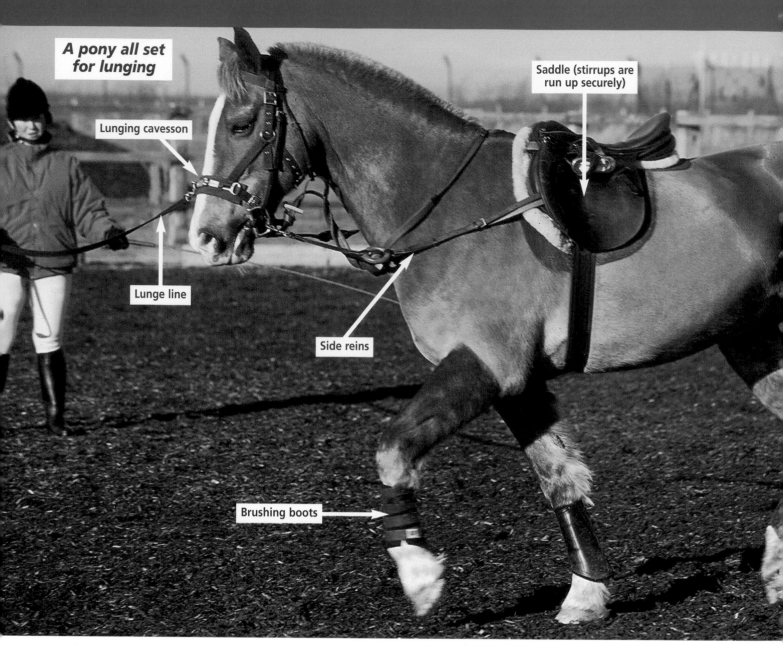

A pony all set
for lunging

Saddle (stirrups are
run up securely)

Lunging cavesson

Lunge line

Side reins

Brushing boots

Taking the lu

When a horse or pony is being trained to accept a rider, lunging is used to develop his suppleness and strength and introduce him first to a handler's commands, then to a rider. It involves sending the horse around a large circle at the end of a long rein.

In fact, lunging is useful at any time to help exercise a horse, polish up his paces, increase relaxation and suppleness, or to help teach a novice rider.

Uncomfortable or badly fitting tack during lunging is not only useless, it could discourage the horse from participating in training at all.

Lunging has its own specialized equipment. It is dangerous to lunge a pony using just an ordinary halter and rope because this gives you no control.

Above: This picture shows how the cavesson goes over the bridle and how the side reins fit. These side reins have rubber ring inserts to allow a little give in the contact. The bridle reins are twisted and looped through the throat-latch to be out of the way.

tack tip

Fit a cavesson snugly so that it cannot be pulled across the horse's eye on the side of the head to the outside of the lunging circle.

Lunging cavesson

A lunging cavesson is a sturdy, well-padded noseband with metal swivel-rings fastened to the front and sides where the lunge rein is attached. A thick throat-latch and jowl strap keep it steady on the head and away from the eyes. The lunge rein is usually fastened to the front ring.

A young pony starts his education using the cavesson by itself. Later, a bit can be added to give him the feel of it in his mouth.

Lunge line

A lunge line is a long, heavy rein, usually made of cotton webbing. There is a buckle or clip set on a swivel at the end that fastens on the cavesson. The other end has a loop, but you should never put your hand through this because it could get caught if the horse or pony pulls away. Usually, the handler will gather the lunge line up in her hands to keep it from dragging on the ground.

Side reins

Side reins are often used for more control and to give a young horse the idea of what a rider's rein contact feels like. Later on in training, they are used to suggest to the horse that he carry his head lower and bring his nose in more. They are not designed to keep the head down. If they are too tight, they only make the horse tense and stiff and discourage him from going forward.

Roller

A heavy roller is sometimes used for lunging, particularly for young horses that have not yet been introduced to a saddle. Lunging rollers have rings on the sides to allow long lines to pass through or side-reins to be attached. The roller must fit snugly, but not too tightly! It is safest to also use a loose breast-collar to keep a roller from slipping back, and a crupper to keep it from slipping forward.

Fitting side reins correctly for a particular horse or pony's level of training is important. Lunging is a skill that must be mastered. If you are thinking of lunging your horse or pony, ask an expert to show you how it's done.

During lunging, your horse or pony needs to wear brushing boots.

nge

Below: Sometimes a lunging roller is used instead of a saddle.

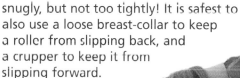

Right: This is how the side reins attach to the girth straps.

More headgear

Halters

There are times when you have to be in control of your pony but don't need to actually use a bridle. Catching, leading to and from the field, or tying up for grooming are all occasions when a halter is used. Whenever you are leading a pony on the road, however, it is best for him to wear a bridle, just in case he is startled. A halter does not give any control over a horse or pony that is frightened.

Halters have a noseband, headpiece, and jowl piece. Some also have a browband. They are usually made of nylon webbing or leather. The problem with nylon is that if, in an emergency, your pony needs to get free from his halter, it simply will not break. If your pony has to have a halter on out in the field, it should be a leather one, not nylon, or have a quick release tab. Check it often to make sure it is not rubbing.

Lead ropes

Lead ropes come in many colors to match the halter. They clip to the halter under the jaw. The least expensive are cotton rope with a spring clip at the end (fasten this away from the head so it doesn't dig in). Also available are tougher ropes made of nylon that come with many different kinds of clips — spring, trigger, or safety. Practice getting these undone quickly in case there is a problem that requires quick action.

Ponies can be led more easily by threading the lead rope through the D-ring on one side of the halter, under the jaw to the opposite D-ring. Alternatively, wrap the rope around the nose (well above the nostrils) and back through the ring under the jaw where it is clipped on.

Above: Use a halter that is the right size for your pony. They come in horse and cob. If it is too loose, it could catch on something and be dangerous. If it is too tight, it will chafe. The noseband should come halfway between the mouth and the face bones.

Above: Foals wear a light halter called a foal slip.

Halters

Halters are a simple form of headgear. They have a rope going over the head and a rope going over the nose, fastened together at the near side in a bound loop. The rope can be slipped through the loop, or more correctly, should be knotted there to keep the halter from being pulled tighter and tighter around the nose. Wide-webbing halters are used for cobs and heavy horses in the show ring.

A rope halter

Above: When you are not using the halter, fasten the lead rope by making a loop, then twisting the rope around it and tucking the end in, *as shown in the two pictures above.*

in-hand bridles

At a show, you might spot various bridles. Each type of class or breed has its own particular one that is correct for that event. It is named accordingly.

Arab bridle

In-hand bridle

Showing halter

All wrapped

Ponies grow very effective winter coats of their own, so why wrap them in blankets? The answer is that, depending on the type of pony you are talking about and the kind of lifestyle he leads, his own fur coat is not always enough to keep him warm.

There is nothing like being cold to make a horse or pony lose weight rapidly and feel completely miserable.

Does your pony need a blanket? He certainly does if you are working him regularly and have had him clipped. Clipping has taken away his own natural protection against the weather, so it is only fair to replace it with a warm blanket. All lightweight types of ponies, like those with quite a lot of Arab or Thoroughbred blood, will also need a blanket in winter. These breeds are suited to live in hot climates — they have fine hair, thin skins, and feel the cold easily.

Invest in at least two outdoor blankets so a spare is always on hand. Even the best blankets get soaked during a downpour. Ponies also have a knack for ripping their blankets or escaping from them and leaving them trampled in the mud.

Above: Most ponies that spend time in the field in winter need a blanket. This blanket is a traditional, canvas New Zealand type.

fitting right

Pictured are two good-quality blankets, one for the stable and one for the field.

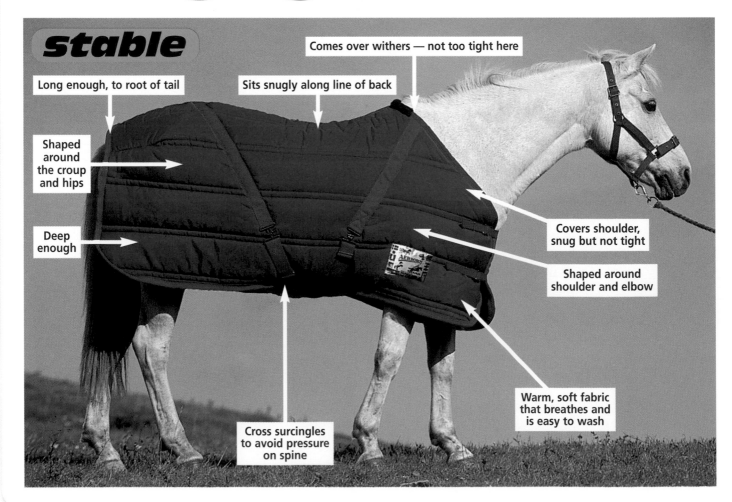

stable

Comes over withers — not too tight here

Long enough, to root of tail

Sits snugly along line of back

Shaped around the croup and hips

Deep enough

Covers shoulder, snug but not tight

Shaped around shoulder and elbow

Cross surcingles to avoid pressure on spine

Warm, soft fabric that breathes and is easy to wash

up

Use your judgment about whether or not to use a blanket. Ponies that live out all or most of the winter need one. Older ponies, too, need a blanket because their internal heating systems do not work as efficiently as they once did.

If your pony is a hardy type that grows a dense coat, if he is not ridden very much in winter and so is not clipped, and if he is fed plenty of hay, he may not need a blanket.

Some people keep a close eye on the weather and only use a blanket when conditions turn bad, particularly when it rains heavily day after day — the type of weather that ponies suffer in the most.

All good owners will check their pony's warmth at every visit and be prepared to put on, or take off, his blankets as necessary to keep him at the most comfortable temperature for the weather conditions that day.

Above: This blanket is too short and too shallow. It has old-fashioned girth surcingles that are tight and restricting around the pony's belly. Blankets that are too small are uncomfortable. Besides causing skin rubs, a tight blanket can prevent a pony from grazing comfortably.

Above: A hand's width should fit between any surcingles or leg straps and the pony.

tack tip

Check body temperature by feeling the base of the ears, belly, flanks, and loins. If they are cold, so is your pony! This is the time to put on a blanket or a thicker one or add an extra layer. Feeding more hay will also warm him up. Being too hot is just as uncomfortable as being too cold. A hot and clammy coat means he is overheating — take the blanket off, or put on a lighter one. Never put a blanket on a pony in warm weather just to keep him clean.

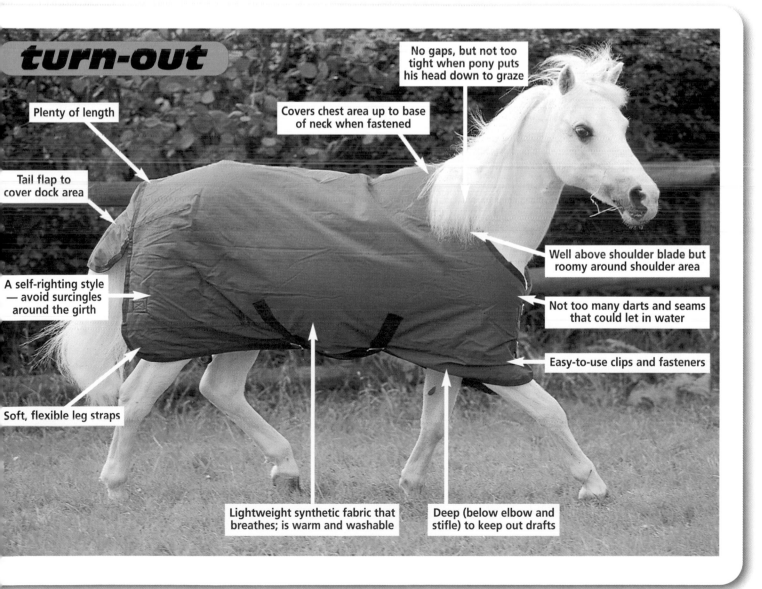

turn-out

- Plenty of length
- Tail flap to cover dock area
- A self-righting style — avoid surcingles around the girth
- Soft, flexible leg straps
- Covers chest area up to base of neck when fastened
- No gaps, but not too tight when pony puts his head down to graze
- Well above shoulder blade but roomy around shoulder area
- Not too many darts and seams that could let in water
- Easy-to-use clips and fasteners
- Lightweight synthetic fabric that breathes; is warm and washable
- Deep (below elbow and stifle) to keep out drafts

Which blanket?

Choosing a turn-out blanket

Blankets designed to be worn by a horse or pony in the field are often called New Zealand blankets, or turn-out blankets.

Buy the best

Think about how much "staying" power your horse or pony's outdoor blanket must have. It has to stay in place when he gallops, bucks, and rolls. It also has to keep him warm and dry in all types of harsh weather. An outdoor blanket has to be tough, especially if your horse or pony is outside much of the time. It must not slip or he will be left unprotected or chafed. Always buy the best you can afford.

Materials

Some of the inexpensive New Zealand blankets are not very well designed. They may have flimsy fasteners or old-fashioned surcingles around the girth that are very uncomfortable for a horse or pony to wear all day long. It is well worth saving for a top-quality blanket. Although the traditional canvas is still widely used, modern synthetic fabrics are best. Synthetic blankets are light in weight even when wet. They dry quickly and keep the rain out and the warmth in, without letting the pony get too hot. Some reflect a pony's body heat back to him. Others are able to draw away any moisture on the body through the fabric into the air, so you can put a blanket on a pony damp from sweat or rain and know that he won't catch a chill.

Good blankets are designed to stay on a pony, no matter what his activity level, with a minimum of straps. These may be cross-surcingles, front leg straps, back leg straps, or a combination of each.

Fasteners

Think of yourself, too. Your frozen fingers on a cold, dark winter's night don't work well. When purchasing a blanket, look for clips and straps that are quick and easy to fasten, even in the cold and dark of night. They shouldn't quickly clog with mud or become rusty. They should clean easily.

Above: Look for straps and fasteners that are easy to use.

Above and below: Take careful measurements to get the right blanket.

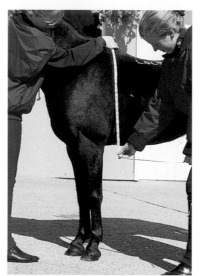
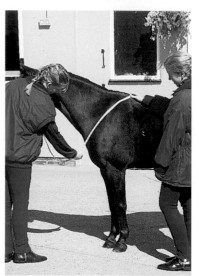

sizes

Blankets range in size from about 4 feet (1.2 m) in length for a small pony to 9 feet (2.8 m) for a large horse. They increase in size by 2-inch (5-cm) stages.

tack tip *Most turn-out blankets have back leg straps like this. Loop them through each other before fastening to avoid chafing between the legs. Also available are blankets with a "spider" arrangement of straps underneath the belly.*

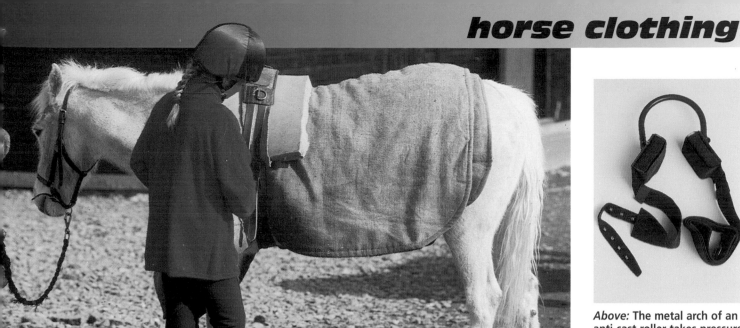

Above: The metal arch of an anti-cast roller takes pressure off the back and keeps the horse from rolling over in his stable and getting stuck.

Above: Pictured is an old-fashioned jute blanket with a roller. Avoid using a roller if you can because it is not comfortable for the horse. Rollers should always be padded so there is no pressure on the spine.

tack tip

Friction around the shoulders can often cause rubbing, especially with a sensitive-skinned pony. First, check that the blanket fits as well as possible around this area. You might want to buy him one of the new under-blanket shoulder bibs.

Choosing a stable blanket

Even though your pony might be in the shelter of his stable, he may still need a blanket. In the field, he hopefully can move around to find shelter and keep his temperature up. Inside, his freedom is restricted, so you must make sure he doesn't get cold standing still.

Styles

Most of today's indoor blankets are made of quilted, synthetic fabrics that are easy to wash and wear. They come in various thicknesses. Most have a tough, synthetic fabric on the outside with a softer cotton lining on the inside.

Again, buy the best you can. For a pony that is clipped, in particular, it is worth the money for one good, thick stable blanket, rather than struggling with lots of thin layers.

tack fact

In years gone by, horses had two blankets for the stable. A jute blanket was used at night when the blanket was likely to get dirty. In the morning, it was replaced with a beautiful wool day blanket.

Fasteners

Today's stable blankets usually have either cross-surcingles or are so well designed that they need only back leg straps to keep them in place.

Doubling up

Turn-out and stable blankets rolled into one are now available. These combination blankets can be very useful — but remember, you should still remove and replace the blanket of a horse or pony that is in the field at least once a day. Never leave a blanket on your horse or pony for days without looking underneath!

Above: Owners of mudlark ponies can invest in a hood to keep grime off their pony. It goes right over the head. Make sure it is a good fit to avoid rubbing when the pony grazes. A hood is not a good idea for a horse or pony that lives out all the time.

Clothing to cool or

A turn-out and a stable blanket are the two items every pony needs. Even if your pony usually lives out without a blanket, it is smart to have them on hand in case of very bad weather or if he needs to be brought in due to an emergency.

There are several other types of blankets and sheets you might want to add to your pony's collection.

Anti-sweat sheets and coolers

The purpose of lightweight, anti-sweat sheets is to cool down and dry off a horse or pony that is wet from sweat, rain, or a bath. Without them, the horse or pony could catch a chill and become ill. Warm air gets trapped within a mesh and is held close to the horse or pony. Of course, this can only happen if the air pockets truly are trapped. Coolers, which are more expensive, do this automatically.

If you are using the anti-sweat version, you will need to put another blanket on top. This might be a summer sheet in warm weather, a travel blanket when traveling, or a stable blanket in winter.

At shows and events, look for a variety of coolers. The American-style coolers extend up the neck, fasten to the halter, and extend down to the knee and hock level. They are particularly good for drying a hot, sweaty horse in cold weather.

Above: **This pony is wearing a mesh anti-sweat sheet that works only if it has another light blanket on top to trap pockets of warm air.**

tack tip

Keep the lining of a stable blanket clean longer by placing an old summer sheet underneath it. Fasten the cross-surcingles snugly to keep everything in place.

putting on/taking off blankets

Practice putting on and taking off blankets carefully so as not to frighten your pony. All types of blankets are handled in the same way from either side of the pony.

1 Fold the back half over the front and hold it off the ground. Place it carefully over the pony's back, well forward.

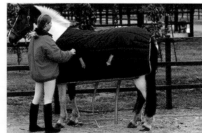

2 Slide it back a little, so the hair underneath lies smoothly. Fold the back half down to the top of the tail and smooth it.

3 Secure the front fasteners first, then work backward until all are secure. The width of your hand should easily fit underneath cross-surcingles and between all leg straps and the pony.

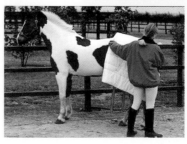

4 To take a blanket off, undo any hind leg straps first. Then undo the front breast straps. Leave any surcingles or rollers until last. Take hold of the back seam and slide it off toward the tail. Fold it neatly with the lining on the inside so it doesn't get covered in dirt, straw, or shavings.

be cozy

Below: This cotton cooler works without an extra sheet.

Above: Be ready for the rain with an exercise or rain sheet.

Summer sheets

You might wonder why a pony would ever need to wear a blanket in hot weather. It keeps the dust off a freshly groomed coat and gives the horse some relief from flies. Summer sheets usually need to be fastened with a surcingle.

Travel blanket

Beautiful, showy travel blankets will make your horse or pony look elegant.

Exercise sheets and rain sheets

These are short blankets that cover the horse's loins and hindquarters. They keep these areas warm and dry during exercise on cold or wet days. The sheets are waterproof and made of nylon, waxed cotton, or wool. They come in fluorescent fabric to make the horse or pony extra visible for safety.

Use one whenever there are rain clouds on the horizon — it can save hours of waiting for a wet pony to dry before being able to put his blanket back on again. Most exercise sheets have built-in loops and straps to keep them in place. Remember to pull the sheet up into the saddle gullet, just like a saddle pad.

tack tip

No exercise sheet? Use an old stable blanket with the fasteners removed. Fold the front smoothly underneath the girth to keep it securely under the saddle.

using under-blankets

These days, most stable blankets are warm enough and don't need extra layers underneath. Even so, it is worth knowing how to put on an under-blanket correctly in case you ever want to add more warmth to an old-fashioned blanket. The under-blanket must be fastened securely using a roller or padded surcingle. If it slips back, it will be useless and very uncomfortable for the horse or pony.

1 Fold the under-blanket in half and place it on top of the pony.

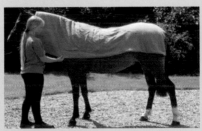

2 Fold it back to cover the quarters *(pictured above).*

3 Take the front corners and fold them up to the withers.

4 Now put the outer blanket on top.

5 Fold the front *V* of the blanket over the top *(pictured above).*

6 Fasten the roller around the girth, making sure the blanket is lying flat underneath.

Looking after legs

With four long legs, it is not surprising that horses and ponies often get knocks, cuts, and bruises on their lower legs and heels. Poor conformation causes some horses and ponies to move their opposite legs too closely together and to knock one into the other. This is called interference. Interference can also be caused by moving in an unbalanced way (particularly in young horses), fatigue, stumbling, galloping in muddy conditions, and poor riding.

Bumps can also happen when jumping — either from hitting a pole or scraping the forelegs with the hind legs upon landing. Each type of interference has a name, depending on where it is on the leg:

Brushing On the inside of the leg, below the knee.

Speedy-cutting On the inside or back of the leg, above the knee.

Over-reaching On the back of the tendon, pastern, or heels.

Tread When the horse treads on itself or another horse.

Injuries to the lower legs take a long time to heal and can easily get infected. It is wise to avoid injury completely by fitting the horse or pony with boots.

Above: Knocks and scrapes to the legs can easily happen, especially during some of the more active sports. A few minutes spent putting on boots can save on an expensive vet bill.

when to use boots

- ♦ During normal exercise, if your pony does not have a very straight action
- ♦ Schooling a youngster
- ♦ Jumping
- ♦ Lunging
- ♦ Traveling

tack tip

You may decide not to use boots if you are going to spend a long day riding in muddy conditions. Sometimes grit and mud can grind down inside the boots and rub the legs very sore.

boot-fitting checklist

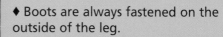
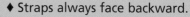

- ♦ Boots are always fastened on the outside of the leg.
- ♦ Straps always face backward.
- ♦ Fit the right boots to the right legs — front and hind pairs are usually shaped differently, and hinds generally have more straps.
- ♦ Fasten snugly, but not too tightly.
- ♦ Fasten the center buckle/strap first, then the one below, then the top one, to keep the boot from slipping down the leg and frightening the pony
- ♦ To undo, release the top strap first.

What are boots made of?

All boots used to be made of leather. Many of today's boots are made of high-tech materials. These are comfortable, good at absorbing shock, and easy to wash. Some still have the old-fashioned straps and buckles. Others have Velcro, which is very handy but needs to be kept clean and free of straw in order to work properly.

tack tip

Before putting rubber bell boots on, it helps to warm the rubber first so that it stretches. Hold your pony's front hoof securely between your legs, just like the farrier does. With the boot inside out and the bottom edge nearest you, grip hard and pull this edge over the foot. Once it is over the pastern, turn it the right way around and make sure it is not on so tightly that it rubs.

Above: Stretch the bell boot over the foot and make sure it is not too tight.

learn all about... protective boots

brushing and bell boots

fetlock boots

Fetlock boots are short boots that cover the inside of the fetlock joint only.

Yorkshire boots are rectangles of heavy, felt cloth that tie around the leg above the fetlock and fold down double to cover the entire fetlock joint. Usually used only on hind legs for horses that brush out slightly.

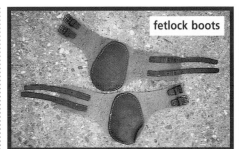

Yorkshire boot

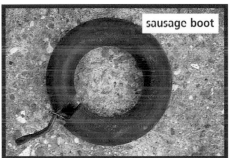

sausage boot

knee boot

Brushing boots fit around the entire leg, protecting from below the knee to above the fetlock. Extra padding protects the inside of the leg. Gives all-around protection for exercising, schooling, and jumping.

Speedy-cut boots are extra-long brushing boots that cover the inside of the knee/hock. Often used for galloping. There are also extra-long, heavy-duty versions of these boots specially designed for polo.

Tendon boots are open at the front, with padding mainly at the back of the leg to protect the tendons. Mainly used for jumping. Some boots are brushing and tendon boots combined, with padding all around the sides and back.

tendon boot

Sausage boots Two kinds of boots have this name. One is a rubber ring (shown above) that fastens around the pastern or above the fetlock to prevent interference there. The other is a thick, padded ring that fits around the pastern of a foreleg to keep it from scraping the elbow when the horse lies down.

Bell boots pull on over the hoof and fasten around the pastern. Bell boots protect the sensitive coronet and heels from being struck. They are good for jumping and traveling. The bell boot pictured at right is made up of a ring of flaps. These are great for cross-country when the bell-type boots tend to flip inside-out about halfway around the course. If the horse or pony damages a section, only one or two of the flaps will need replacing.

Coronet boots are circular leather boots that fit around the pastern to protect the coronet only.

Knee boots are often called knee caps or skeleton knee boots. They have a padded front to stop damage to the horse's knees if he falls. They fit firmly above the knee, but the lower strap must stay loose to allow the knee to flex. Knee boots for travel cover more of the joint than regular knee boots.

Hock boots are similar to knee boots but are designed to protect the hocks.

bell boot

Left: Avoid bending down in front of the pony's leg like this, in case he moves suddenly.

Bandage business

tack tip

Don't leave exercise bandages on too long, especially if they have become damp or wet. Remove the bandages carefully by passing each bandage from hand to hand as you unwind. Then gently massage each leg to get the circulation going again.

Exercise bandages

An alternative to the boot for leg protection is the exercise bandage. Bandages give the legs support, but boots are best for young riders.

Boots are much quicker and easier than bandages to put on correctly. A poor-fitting bandage can be incredibly painful for a pony and may cause lasting damage to his leg. If you are thinking of using exercise bandages, ask someone experienced to watch you practice until you have perfected the skill. Exercise bandages are made of stretchy cotton fabric, about 2 inches (5 cm) wide and 6.5 feet (2 m) long. They fasten with tapes, Velcro, or clips.

♦ Always use padding underneath a bandage, already cut to the right size for your pony's leg. Padding evens out the pressure and adds protection, warmth, and support. The padding can be traditional Gamgee (soft cotton-wool lined with gauze), although this gets dirty very quickly. Reusable choices include synthetic Fybagee or special spongy, shock-absorbing shells that mold to fit around the tendons. These are often used for cross-country.

Putting on exercise bandages

♦ The bandage goes from below the knee to above the fetlock. It must not interfere with the movement of the joints.

♦ Wrap the padding around the leg. Unravel about 4 inches (10 cm) of bandage. Hold it at an angle against the leg below the knee.

♦ Wrap around once to secure the bandage. Then wrap down the leg using firm, but even, pressure. Cover about two-thirds of the previous wrap with each turn. Don't wrap too tightly or too loosely. A tight bandage will damage the leg. A loose one could slip down.

♦ Stop bandaging above the fetlock and work upward again to finish.

♦ Fasten the bandage on the outside of the leg, never on the inside or the front or back. If tapes are used, make sure they lie flat before tying in a double bow and tucking in the ends. The ties can then be stitched or taped over for security. The tape and ties should not be tighter than the bandage itself or they will dig into the leg.

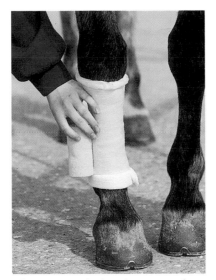

tack tip

Plastic insulation tape helps secure other types of tape or Velcro fasteners on boots or bandages for extra security.

Above: Wrap the bandage around using firm, even pressure.

Above: Never put on a bandage without padding underneath.

Stable bandages

Stable bandages are thicker, wider, and longer than exercise bandages, and they are usually made of stretchy fabric. They are not used for riding but to give warmth and support in the stable to tired or injured legs. Stable bandages are also used for protection when traveling and for first-aid. Stable bandages cover more of the leg than exercise bandages, reaching from just below the knee or hock down over the fetlock to the coronet.

tack tip

Never kneel on the floor to put bandages on — what if the pony moves suddenly? Always crouch down so you can spring up quickly if necessary.

putting on stable bandages

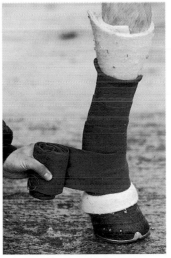

tack tip

If you have bandaged an injury, bandage the opposite leg, too. It is taking a lot of extra strain and needs support.

tack tip

Wet legs can be dried quickly with stable bandages over dry straw. This is called thatching.

1 Wrap padding around the leg. For traveling, give your pony extra protection by wrapping padding over the knee or hock and the coronet. Unravel about 3 inches (8 cm) of bandage. Hold it at an angle against the outside of the leg. Wrap once around the leg, tucking in the end as you go. Roll evenly down the leg, so each turn comes about halfway down the previous one.

2 Wind over the fetlock and pastern at an angle, then start going upward again, finishing halfway up the cannon bone.

3 Fasten securely, making sure ties are not twisted and are knotted in a bow with ends tucked safely in.

tack tip

Keep bandages clean. When you take them off, roll them up tightly and evenly, with no wrinkles, so they go back on the leg smoothly. When you roll up a bandage, start with the outside pointed end. Lay the tapes or Velcro flat and roll them into the inside — that way they will be in position for next time.

Traveling in

A horse trailer can be an uncomfortable, scary, and dangerous place for a horse or pony to be. Traveling in it is a completely foreign experience that goes against his nature. Do everything you can to make sure he travels safely and happily. Use the appropriate equipment.

blanket
Whatever the weather, a blanket or sheet protects against scratches, rubs, flies, dust, and drafts. On hot days, a cotton summer sheet is ideal. In winter, use a stable blanket or wool travel or day blanket. A roller or surcingle, with padding at the spine, should be used to make sure there is no slipping. A breast-collar should also be used so that the roller does not move backward.

tail protection
You may wonder why a pony's tail needs guarding against damage. Think how ponies like to lean against the trailer ramp to help balance themselves. It only takes a few minutes to rub the top of a tail raw.

The very least your pony should travel in is a well-secured tail bandage. Cover tail-rubbers with tail guards. These are made of tough fabric that fastens around the top of the tail with tapes, straps, or Velcro. A long tape goes along the back to the roller to keep the bandage in place. If you want to keep your pony's tail extra clean, you could put it into a tail bag, which secures the tail in the same way.

leg protection
Although you can use stable bandages together with knee/hock boots and over-reach boots to protect the legs, good travel boots do all of this at once. Travel boots are soft and flexible leggings. They contain a thick layer of padding covered with a synthetic or tough cotton outer layer. They usually have Velcro fasteners.

tack tip

Tail bandages are also used to keep a stabled horse's tail tidy after grooming. They should never be put on damp or left on for more than a few hours.

tack tip

Guard against overheating by using an anti-sweat sheet under the blanket/summer sheet. Fold the top layer back at the shoulder and secure it with a padded roller or surcingle. This pony (right) is wearing knee and hock boots for traveling.

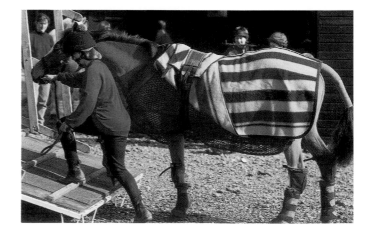

style

halter & lead rope

To lead the pony in and tie him up inside.

tack tip

Choose travel boots carefully and get a good fit for your pony. Too big and baggy, and they will slip down. Too small, and his leg won't be fully protected. The right size should reach well over the knees and hocks, fit snugly around the leg, and cover the coronet at the bottom. Buy sturdy boots with plenty of padding.

Travel gear

poll guard

This shaped and toughened hat is secured to the halter. It is a sensible precaution if your pony tends to throw his head in the air when loading or unloading or during traveling. It protects the sensitive poll.

putting on a tail bandage

A tail bandage is like an exercise bandage. This is how to put one on:

1 Stand behind but slightly to the side of your pony and dampen the tail with a water brush. Gently lift the tail. If the pony clamps his tail down, wait for him to relax. Try putting the tail over your shoulder to keep it out of the way.

2 Unravel some of the bandage, and slip it under the tail. Put the outside of the roll of bandage nearest the tail, to get the tension right. Place the end at an angle.

3 Make one wrap around, fold the end down, and wrap around again. Smooth the hair underneath.

4 Continue wrapping, keeping the bandage firm and even. Go about halfway down each previous wrap, keeping it smooth with no turned-under edges.

5 When you reach the end of the dock bone, start going up again. Finish mid-way up the tail. Tie the tapes securely in a knotted bow and tuck in the ends. Bend the tail gently back into shape.

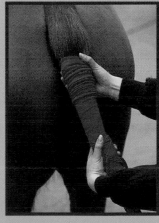

6 To take a tail bandage off, don't unwind it the total length. Simply untie the tapes, take hold of the top, and pull down firmly so the bandage comes off the tail in one piece.

Taking care of tack

H orse and pony tack does not last forever. If you take care of it, however, it will last a long time. It will also keep you and your horse or pony out of dangerous situations. Dry, cracked leather can snap without warning. Rotten, frayed stitching can break at any moment. Even metal parts weaken or get sharp and could break and injure you and your pony. Torn blankets with holes in them let in the cold, and a leg could get caught in them. Hard, stiff leather — or saddle pads and bandages caked with grease or dry sweat — soon rub a pony and make him sore, uncomfortable, and unhappy. Make a resolution now to take care of your tack.

Above: It's not surprising that New Zealand blankets need a good washing and overhauling at the end of winter!

Blankets

Unless you have a huge washing machine, it is less expensive and easier to send blankets away to a service to be cleaned. Your stable blanket may fit in the machine at home, but read the washing instructions on the blanket first to see if it should be machine washed.

Above: You can also sometimes hose and scrub blankets down.

Saddle pads, girths, and halters

Most saddle pads can be washed in a machine. However, pure sheepskin needs to be brushed, and gel pads need to be sponged clean.

Cotton-padded girths can go in the wash. Pop the nylon halter in, too. You can buy special tabs to protect the machine from the clanking of the buckles, or slip the tack into a big pillowcase. Leather girths, halters, and boots need regular saddle soaping.

Bandages and boots

Travel boots, bandages, and synthetic boots can also be machine-washed. Put them in a pillowcase to prevent tangling.

tack tips

Remember, canvas New Zealand blankets need scrubbing and reproofing after winter.

*

If you are washing tack at home, don't use the types of detergents that may bother your pony's skin.

*

After winter, clean your blankets and have any tears repaired. Don't put them away dirty and dig them out in September and expect to be ready to go.

Above: These girls are cleaning their bridles without taking them apart. Take your bridle apart for a thorough cleaning once a week.

Above: After you have finished with it, put all your tack away.

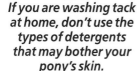

tack fact

The little lumps of black grease that build up on leather are called jockeys. Pick them off with a blunt knife or coin. In the old days, people rubbed them off with horsehair.

Wash the bit off each time you untack, so it never gets caked with dry saliva and food.

❋

Check for fraying or rotting stitching, cracks in leather, or other signs of wear and tear.

❋

If your tack is wet through, quickly put on some leather dressing or neatsfoot oil to keep it supple as it dries out.

❋

Never put wet leather near a radiator or fire because it will dry too quickly and become brittle.

❋

If the tack is really greasy, add a tiny squirt of dishwashing liquid to the water.

❋

If you need to store your saddle, bridle, or other gear for a long time, make sure they are very clean. Then wrap them in a pillowcase. Put saddles on a rack, and lay bridle straps out flat. Avoid plastic bags because these get damp inside and make the leather moldy.

❋

Put plenty of soap, or even some oil, into the turns in the leather and areas that take a lot of pressure — such as the girth straps, where the reins turn around the bit rings, and where the stirrup irons sit on the stirrup leathers. Use a toothbrush to get into tight places.

Saddle and bridle

All your leather tack, including the saddle and bridle, is cleaned in much the same way. Most leather cleaning products are still based on the traditional glycerine saddle soap. Try to clean your tack every time you use it, or at least once a week.

You will need:

♦ A bucket of lukewarm water.
♦ Two sponges or cloths — one for wiping and one for soaping.
♦ Soft cloth for polishing.
♦ Saddle soap.
♦ An old toothbrush.

This is what you do:

1 Undo all buckles and take off the girth and stirrup leathers. Put the stirrup irons and bit into a bucket of warm water. Scrub them with a toothbrush.

♦ Clean and soap straight straps by putting them on a hook or holding them tightly in one hand and running the cloth down them.

♦ A saddle is best cleaned on a saddle horse, but you can hold it on your lap or the back of a chair.

2 Wet the cloth or sponge in lukewarm water. Wring it out and gently wipe all over every strap and piece of leather. Pay extra attention to areas that get greasy, such as under nosebands, girths, and the back edges of the saddle. Don't get the leather too wet! Avoid scratching it if the tack is very muddy.

3 Now for the soaping. The golden rule is, "never wet the sponge or you will end up with nothing but bubbles." Dip the bar of soap in warm water. Now rub the sponge on it, and work the soap into the leather. Give the underside  (the rougher side) of all your leather tack plenty because it is the most absorbent. Any soap stuck in buckle holes can be poked through with a toothpick.

♦ For an extra sparkle, shine metal parts with polish. Never put polish on the bit mouthpiece, though. That would taste terrible! Finally, put everything back together again and put it away carefully. Don't forget to switch the right and left stirrup leathers with each cleaning so that they stretch evenly.

♦ Once a month or so, oil leather to condition it. Brush the oil on, avoiding the stitching and the saddle seat where it will smear your clothes and make the seat slippery.

Synthetic saddles

Synthetic saddles are easy to keep clean. Simply brush dry mud off with a dandy brush. Then wipe the saddle all over with lukewarm water and soap.

Glossary

action — the way a bit works in a horse or pony's mouth.

aids — signals given by a rider to communicate with a horse or pony.

bars — the gap at the sides of the mouth where there are no teeth, where the bit lies.

billet — a piece of iron or steel.

bit — the piece of the bridle that is held in the horse or pony's mouth, usually made of metal. The reins are attached to the bit. They are the rider's means of giving hand aids to the horse or pony.

boots — padded protection for a horse or pony's lower legs.

bosal — a simple rope bitless bridle that is used to train young horses and novice riders in Western riding.

breastplate — a type of neckstrap that fastens to the saddle, either at the *D*-rings or the girth straps, and goes between the legs to the girth. It is designed to keep the saddle in place on horses or ponies with a narrow or fit, lean body. In Western riding, it is known as a breastcollar.

bridle — headgear on a horse or pony that carries the bit and reins.

bridoon — a thin snaffle bit with small rings that forms part of a double bridle.

browband — the section of the bridle that comes across the forehead, below the ears.

brushing — poor leg action, where one foot knocks against the opposite lower leg as the horse or pony moves.

cantle — the back of a saddle.

cavesson — a simple type of plain noseband; special headgear with rings attached to the noseband for securing a lunge line.

cheekpieces — straps in the bridle that run down either side of the pony's face and hold the bit in the mouth.

cheeks — sections of a bit that extend beyond the bit rings, either above or below the mouthpiece (or both).

cinch — the name given to the girths on a Western saddle. The front cinch holds the saddle in place, while the back, or flank, cinch keeps it from tipping forward during cattle roping.

cob — a stocky, short-legged riding horse.

conformation — the overall shape and appearance of a horse or pony.

coronet — the lower part of the pastern (the part of the foot from the fetlock to the top of the hoof).

crupper — a broad strap that attaches to the saddle, with a padded ring at the end that the tail goes through. It keeps the saddle from slipping forward.

curb — the general name for any type of bit with cheeks and a curb chain that works with a lever action.

curb chain — a short chain or strap that attaches to either side of a curb bit. It lies in the curb groove, behind the pony's chin, and tightens as the bottom rein is used.

D-ring — a *D*-shaped metal piece on a saddle that is used for attaching breastplates, saddlebags, and cruppers; a particular shape of bit ring.

domesticated — the condition of being tamed.

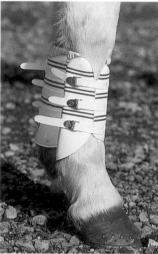

Above: Boots protect a horse or pony's legs from knocks and scrapes.

Below: Many ponies need a particular bit when jumping cross-country.

dressage — the execution by a horse or pony of precision movements in response to signals from a rider.

eggbutt — a *T*-shaped joint between the mouthpiece and rings of a bit that keeps the lips of the horse or pony from being pinched.

equitation — the art of riding on horseback.

farrier — a professional trained to care for and fit shoes on a horse or pony's feet.

fetlock — the projection on the back of a horse or pony's leg above the hoof.

fly link — an extra-large part in the center of a curb chain where the lip strap passes through.

foal — any young horse or pony up to the age of one year.

gag — a bit family that combines action on the horse's mouth with pressure on the poll but has no curb chain.

girth — the strap that encircles the chest of a horse or pony to secure the saddle on his back.

Grakle — a drop-type noseband with narrow straps that cross over at the front of the nose.

hackamore — any bitless bridle; but more correctly, only the Western rope bosal bridle is a true hackamore.

halter — headgear made of a noseband, headpiece, and throat-latch. It is usually used for leading and tying up.

head stall — the bridle in Western riding. There is no noseband, and often no browband or throat-latch. The bridle is made up of the bit and a slip-head.

horse — a large hoofed animal of the Equidae family that is over 14.2 hands high. A hand equals 4 inches (10.2 centimeters)

in-hand bridle — a simple bridle where the noseband is attached directly to the cheekpieces. It is usually used with a chain link lead rein for show classes where the horse or pony is not ridden (therefore, in-hand).

interference — the situation when a horse or pony knocks one leg against the other.

jute — an old-fashioned, tough sacking material that is still used in certain blankets.

keepers — the small leather loops that hold the ends of the bridle straps neatly in place.

Kimblewick — a type of Pelham bit that is used with single reins.

lunge line — a long rein that is used in the training of a horse or pony to provide some control of the animal.

lunging — an exercise used in training horses and riders. The horse moves in large circles around a handler, controlled by a lunge line.

martingale — a neckstrap that is attached between the forelegs to the girth and also the reins or a cavesson noseband, to give the rider more control of the horse or pony.

mullen-mouth — a type of bit mouthpiece that has no joint but is slightly curved.

near side — the left-hand side of a horse or pony.

neckstrap — a long, leather strap that goes around a horse or pony's neck for a novice rider to hold onto for a little extra security.

New Zealand blanket — a canvas blanket for outdoors.

noseband — a part of the bridle that goes around the nose, either above (cavesson) or below (dropped) the bit.

off side — the right-hand side of a horse or pony.

pastern — the part of a horse or pony's foot that extends from the fetlock to the top of the hoof.

Pelham — a type of curb bit that works like a double bridle but has only one mouthpiece.

poll — the top or back of the head of a horse or pony behind the ears.

Above: **Western equitation has its own special tack that is different from the tack used in English-style riding.**

Below: **In winter weather, a New Zealand blanket will keep a horse or pony warm.**

pommel — the front arch of a saddle.

pony — a large hoofed animal of the Equidae family that is under 14.2 hands high. A hand equals 4 inches (10.2 cm).

roller — a wide strap used around the belly to keep a blanket in place on a horse or pony.

saddle pad — a shaped pad made of cotton or fleece used under the saddle of a horse or pony to ease pressure and absorb sweat.

slip-head — a long, narrow strap that holds the noseband of a bridle up, or the bridoon bit in a double bridle.

snaffle — the largest, simplest, and most commonly seen family of bits, usually having one ring on either side of the mouthpiece.

stirrup — a metal ring that hangs on a strap from a saddle. It supports the rider's foot.

surcingle — a narrow, stretchy strap that is placed over a saddle in cross-country competitions for extra security or placed around the horse or pony's belly to fasten a blanket in place.

tack — stable gear or harness equipment, such as a saddle and bridle, used on a horse or pony.

throat-latch — the thin strap that passes under the jowl to prevent the bridle from easily being pulled over the ears. The cheekpieces attach to the throat-latch.

under-blanket — a thin blanket that fits underneath a stable blanket for extra warmth.

Western riding — a style of riding where horses and ponies change direction in response to pressure on their necks and do halts at the touch of curb bits.

Weymouth — a type of curb bit often used in a double bridle.

For Further Study

Books

Basic Tack. Vanessa Briton (Crowood Press)

Fitting Tack. Jane Holderness-Roddam (Half Halt Press)

Great American Horses (series). Victor Gentle and Janet Perry (Gareth Stevens)

Horses. Animal Families (series). (Gareth Stevens)

Horses and Tack. M. E. Ensminger (Houghton Mifflin)

The Illustrated Guide to Horse Tack. Susan McBane (Storey Books)

Magnificent Horses of the World (series). Schrenk/Micek (Gareth Stevens)

The New Book of Saddlery and Tack. Carolyn Henderson (Howell Book House)

The Saddle Club (series). Bonnie Bryant (Gareth Stevens)

Saddlery and Horse Equipment. Sarah Muir (Lorenz Books)

Tack. Cherry Hill (Storey Books)

Tack Buyer's Guide. Charlene Strickland (Breakthrough)

Treasured Horses (series). (Gareth Stevens)

The Wonder of Wild Horses. Animal Wonders (series). Mark Henckel (Gareth Stevens)

Above: Be sure to choose the tack that is a perfect fit for your horse or pony.

Videos

America's Wild Horses. (Wolfgang Bayer Productions)

Horses. (Goldhil Home Media)

Horses: A to Z. (Third Coast Entertainment)

Horses: To Care Is To Love. (AIMS Media)

The Little Horse That Could. (Tapeworm)

Monty Roberts: A Real Horse Whisperer. (Twentieth Century Fox)

Pony Tales. (Publishers' Choice Video)

The Science of Riding. (Discovery Trail)

Web Sites

www.freerein.com/guide/

horses.product.com/

members.tripod.com/~HoofBeat/home.html

24.138.3.145/toppage13.htm

stormz.com/bridle

www.horses-tack.com/

Some web sites stay current longer than others. For further web sites, use your search engines to locate the following topics: *horse care, saddlery, tack,* and *wild horses.*

Index

bandages 56, 57, 58, 59, 60

bits 4, 5, 15, 20, 21, 22, 23, 24, 25, 26, 27, 28, 29, 30, 31, 32, 33, 34, 35, 36, 37, 38, 39, 40, 41, 42, 43, 45, 61

blankets 4, 15, 48, 49, 50, 51, 52, 53, 58, 60

boots 5, 44, 45, 54, 55, 56, 59, 60

bridles 5, 15, 20, 21, 23, 24, 26, 28, 29, 30, 31, 32, 34, 35, 36, 37, 39, 40, 41, 44, 46, 47, 60, 61

browbands 20, 35, 38, 39, 46

care of tack 60, 61

cavesson nosebands 20, 32, 38, 42, 44, 45

cruppers 4, 19, 45

curb bits 21, 22, 23, 26, 27, 28, 29, 31, 33

girths 5, 6, 8, 12, 13, 15, 17, 18, 19, 42, 43, 45, 49, 50, 53, 60, 61

halters 5, 36, 37, 44, 46, 47, 52, 59, 60

head stalls 20, 37, 39

leg protection 9, 54, 55, 56, 57, 58

lunging 44, 45

martingales 4, 32, 40, 42, 43

nosebands 20, 21, 31, 32, 33, 35, 36, 37, 38, 39, 40, 42, 45, 46, 61

Pelhams 4, 21, 23, 26, 27, 41

reins 5, 15, 20, 22, 23, 24, 25, 26, 27, 28, 29, 30, 31, 33, 34, 36, 37, 39, 40, 42, 43, 44, 45, 61

saddle pads 5, 15, 18, 19, 53, 60

saddles 5, 6-19, 44, 45, 53, 61

secondhand tack 15

snaffles 4, 20, 21, 22, 23, 24, 25, 26, 27, 28, 30, 33, 41

stirrups 5, 6, 7, 9, 12, 15, 16, 19, 21, 44, 61

surcingles 17, 49, 50, 51, 52, 53, 58

teeth 36, 37, 38, 40, 41, 42

throat-latches 20, 36, 37, 38, 44, 45

traveling tack 58, 59